History of New Zealand

Good Military Story About Naval in New Zealand

(A Captivating Guide to the History of the Land of the Long White Cloud)

Thomas Estrada

Published By **George Denver**

Thomas Estrada

All Rights Reserved

History of New Zealand: Good Military Story About Naval in New Zealand (A Captivating Guide to the History of the Land of the Long White Cloud)

ISBN   978-1-7781462-7-5

No part of this guidebook shall be reproduced in any form without permission in writing from the publisher except in the case of brief quotations embodied in critical articles or reviews.

Legal & Disclaimer

The information contained in this book is not designed to replace or take the place of any form of medicine or professional medical advice. The information in this book has been provided for educational & entertainment purposes only.

The information contained in this book has been compiled from sources deemed reliable, and it is accurate to the best of the Author's knowledge; however, the Author cannot guarantee its accuracy and validity and cannot be held liable for any errors or omissions. Changes are periodically made to this book. You must consult your doctor or get professional medical advice before using any of the suggested remedies, techniques, or information in this book.

Upon using the information contained in this book, you agree to hold harmless the Author from and against any damages, costs, and expenses, including any legal fees potentially resulting from the application of any of the information provided by this guide. This disclaimer applies to any damages or injury caused by the use and application, whether directly or indirectly, of any advice or information presented, whether for breach of contract, tort, negligence, personal injury, criminal intent, or under any other cause of action.

You agree to accept all risks of using the information presented inside this book. You need to consult a professional medical practitioner in order to ensure you are both able and healthy enough to participate in this program.

Table Of Contents

Chapter 1: Legends And Mythology 1

Chapter 2: Culture And Traditions 18

Chapter 3: Life In Prehistoric New Zealand 30

Chapter 4: Conflict And Change 44

Chapter 5: The New Zealand Wars 61

Chapter 6: The Canterbury Plains Anglican Faith And Agriculture 78

Chapter 7: The Southern Alps And Fiordland 89

Chapter 8: The Treaty Of Waitangi Revisited 101

Chapter 9: The Maori Settlement 113

Chapter 10: The First Europeans In New Zealand 121

Chapter 11: The Treaty Of Waitangi And The Colony Changes 129

Chapter 12: The New Zealand Wars 136

Chapter 13: The Economic Expansion Of New Zealand 147

Chapter 14: The Liberal Age 156

Chapter 15: Identity Emergence In New Zealand... 160

Chapter 16: The Era Of The Reform Party 163

Chapter 17: New Zealand Goes Into War 169

Chapter 18: Expanding Cultural Diversity And Trade... 176

Chapter 1: Legends And Mythology

In the rich tapestry of New Zealand's records, legends and mythology preserve a unique region. These fascinating memories surpassed down through generations provide insights into the cultural and non secular beliefs of the Māori humans, the indigenous populace of Aotearoa. Through the ones tales, we advantage a glimpse into the origins of the land and its humans, woven with factors of nature, gods, and ancestral heroes.

According to Māori mythology, the appearance of Aotearoa starts with the primal mother and father, Ranginui, the sky father, and Papatūānuku, the earth mom. For countless a long time, they lay locked in a extraordinary embody, growing darkness and stifling their numerous kids. Faced with this entice 22 state of affairs, the children, referred to as gods or atua, embarked on a formidable plan to cut up their mother and father and bring slight and existence to the area.

One of the youngsters, Tāne Mahuta, the god of forests and birds, emerged as a pivotal parent in Māori mythology. Tāne Mahuta undertook a brave adventure to the heavens, wherein he found and retrieved the 3 baskets of facts known as te kete tuauri, te kete tuatea, and te kete aronui. These baskets contained the information critical for the introduction of the sector and its population.

Using this information, Tāne Mahuta crafted the primary female, Hineahuone, from the sacred clay of Papatūānuku. From this union, the number one human beings, Tāne Mahuta's human youngsters, were born. This introduction story suggests the interconnectedness of humans, the herbal international, and the gods, emphasizing the significance of balance and concord in the Māori worldview.

Another outstanding discern in Māori mythology is Maui, a respected demigod stated for his cunning and bravado. Maui is well known for his amazing feats, alongside facet the fishing up of the North Island from the depths of the ocean. Legend has it that Maui and his brothers launched right into a fishing day trip, the use of a powerful jawbone as a hook and a woven line made from the hair in their ancestress. After a fierce battle, Maui's efforts have been rewarded even as he hauled up Te Ika-a-Māui, the fish that could end up the North Island.

The mythology of Aotearoa furthermore consists of the tale of Kupe, a legendary explorer taken into consideration the discoverer of New Zealand. According to Māori culture, Kupe set sail from his native land Hawaiki, an ancestral region in the

Pacific, in pursuit of a large octopus that had caused havoc in his village. After a treacherous voyage, Kupe sooner or later arrived in Aotearoa, following the steering of a paranormal puppy whale. His arrival marked the start of Māori presence in the land.

Legends and mythology preserve to play an essential role in Māori way of life, connecting the past to the triumphing and shaping the Māori worldview. These recollections are preserved and passed down thru oral traditions, making sure their longevity and cultural importance. They function a supply of notion, information, and non secular guidance, reinforcing the values of respect, reciprocity, and guardianship of the land.

The legends and mythology of Aotearoa aren't handiest large to the Māori humans but also provide insights into the land's natural capabilities. The memories provide an explanation for the origins of mountains, rivers, lakes, and particular geographical formations, attributing their introduction to the movements of the gods and ancestral beings. This deep spiritual connection to the land maintains to shape the Māori know-how in their region inside the global and their responsibilities as kaitiaki, or guardians.

Exploring the legends and mythology of Aotearoa gives a window into the wealthy cultural ancient beyond of New Zealand's indigenous people. These tales provide a glimpse into the Māori worldview, their courting with the land, and their reverence for the gods and ancestors. By delving into those reminiscences, we deepen our facts of the origins of Aotearoa and the profound connection amongst its people, nature, and the religious realm.

Ancient Polynesian Voyages: Discovering New Zealand

The exploration and agreement of New Zealand by means of way of the Māori humans is a testament to the historical Polynesian voyaging traditions. These intrepid navigators released into bold trips at some stage in great stretches of the Pacific Ocean, the use of their know-how of celestial navigation, currents, winds, and the conduct of marine existence to manual their manner.

The origins of the Polynesian humans may be traced lower lower back hundreds of years to Southeast Asia, from wherein they launched proper right into a incredible maritime enlargement. Using robust double-hulled canoes referred to as waka, the Polynesians navigated their way across the Pacific, conducting and settling many an extended way-flung islands, inclusive of the islands of Polynesia, Melanesia, and Micronesia.

The discovery and settlement of New Zealand, or Aotearoa as it might grow to be stated, are believed to have occurred between the 9th and thirteenth centuries. These voyages had been no small feat, requiring huge courage, navigational expertise, and a deep information of the natural surroundings. The Polynesian explorers trusted a aggregate of celestial observations, which include the location of stars, the solar, and the motion of ocean swells, to manual them closer to their holiday spot.

One precept posits that the preliminary discovery of New Zealand modified into unintended, as Polynesian navigators might also additionally were blown off direction inside the course of their voyages. However, it is widely ordinary that planned exploration and colonization efforts befell over several centuries. The migration routes observed by means of the ones early voyagers are although a topic of look at and debate among researchers.

One of the primary migration theories is that of the Great Fleet, regarded in Māori manner of lifestyles because the waka hourua. According to this principle, a fleet of canoes carried the ancestors of the Māori people to New Zealand, with every canoe representing a remarkable tribal group. These waka have been said to be captained by means of manner of way of professional navigators and carried families, plants, and animals to establish new settlements in Aotearoa.

The particular kind of waka and the names of the voyaging ancestors range among splendid Māori tribes and regions. Some well-known waka consist of Tainui, Aotea, Takitimu, and Te Arawa. Each waka had its very very personal unique statistics, navigational traditions, and reminiscences of exploration and settlement.

The arrival of those early Polynesian settlers marked a big turning issue inside the records of New Zealand. The inexperienced folks encountered a land teeming with numerous ecosystems, such as dense forests, widespread grasslands, rivers teeming with fish, and an abundance of birdlife. The Māori people tailored to their new surroundings, using the resources available to maintain themselves and set up thriving groups.

The Polynesian voyages to New Zealand not most effective added human agreement but furthermore delivered a rich cultural background to the land. The Māori people brought with them their language, customs, social systems, and religious ideals. They set up kinship ties and fashioned iwi (tribes) that would emerge as the cornerstone of Māori society and identification.

The legacy of the Polynesian voyagers remains deeply ingrained in the material of New Zealand nowadays. The Māori language, arts, and oral traditions continue to be celebrated and handed down via generations, maintaining alive the spirit of exploration and connection to the ancestral roots.

The Polynesian voyages to New Zealand stand as a testomony to the first-rate seafaring competencies and navigational know-how of the historical Polynesians. Their trips throughout the extensive expanse of the Pacific Ocean to discover and settle Aotearoa are a testomony to human ingenuity, bravery, and the enduring human choice to find out and are searching for new horizons.

Early Māori Settlements: The Arrival of Tangata Whenua

The arrival of the Māori humans in New Zealand marked a big financial ruin inside the the united states of the usa's facts. Known due to the fact the Tangata Whenua, which means that "humans of the land" in the Māori language, those early settlers installed thriving businesses and laid the ideas for Māori tradition and traditions that go through to at the present time.

The precise timeline of Māori agreement in New Zealand remains a subject of ongoing research and archaeological research. However, it's far considerably believed that the primary Māori explorers arrived in Aotearoa maximum of the 9th and thirteenth centuries, following ancient Polynesian voyaging traditions. These early voyagers undertook perilous trips in the course of large stretches of the Pacific

Ocean, relying on their navigational abilities and expertise of the natural surroundings to navigate uncharted waters.

Upon their arrival in New Zealand, the Māori humans encountered a land teeming with numerous flora and fauna, rich in natural assets. This fertile land furnished the vital sustenance for the established order of settlements and the development of Māori society. The Māori tailored to their new environment, using the assets to be had to them for food, steady haven, and cultural expression.

The way of settling in New Zealand concerned exploring and figuring out appropriate locations for habitation. The Māori people installation settlements in masses of environments, starting from coastal regions to fertile river valleys and mountainous areas. Each agreement, referred to as a pā, changed into strategically positioned to maximise get proper of entry to to meals belongings, waterways, and protective blessings.

Pā have been fortified villages, often placed on hilltops or promontories, surrounded with the aid of defensive earthworks and palisades. These protecting structures served as safety in the route of potential threats and furnished a experience of safety for the community. The production of pā required terrific collective strive, with community individuals going for walks collectively to assemble and preserve those essential centers of social and cultural lifestyles.

Within the pā, communal sports activities befell, fostering social brotherly love and cultural practices. Whare, or homes, have been built to provide secure haven for households, and communal assembly homes, referred to as wharenui, served as collecting places for vital ceremonies, discussions, and storytelling. The pā became no longer most effective a physical space; it end up the coronary coronary heart of the community, an area wherein traditions have been preserved, facts modified into shared, and relationships had been nurtured.

The Māori humans practiced more than a few subsistence sports to maintain their groups. They were professional hunters, gatherers, and agriculturalists. Gathering kai moana, or seafood, from the encompassing coastal waters modified into a essential part of their weight loss plan. Fishing nets, hooks, and traps were used to seize fish, at the same time as shellfish, seaweed, and extraordinary marine assets supplied additional sustenance.

Inland, the Māori cultivated crops together with kūmara (sweet potato), taro, and yams. These plants were grown in small clearings within the wooded region or in large cultivated fields, referred to as māra kai. The cultivation of plants required information of the land, seasons, and sustainable agricultural practices, ensuring a reliable meals deliver for the network.

The Māori human beings moreover practiced horticulture, cultivating beneficial flora together with harakeke (flax) for weaving, and ti kōuka (cabbage tree) for its flexible uses, along facet meals, remedy, and introduction materials. These practices no longer only furnished crucial property but moreover fostered a deep connection among the human beings and the land, reinforcing the idea of kaitiakitanga, or guardianship of the environment.

Trade and trade finished a vital characteristic in early Māori settlements. The Māori advanced significant networks of exchange, changing goods and assets with neighboring companies. This facilitated the sharing of understanding, cultural practices, and valuable materials, in addition improving the interconnectedness of Māori society.

As the Māori settlements grew, so did their social systems and governance systems. Leadership roles, along with rangatira (chiefs) and tohunga (spiritual leaders), emerged to guide and uphold the traditions and values of the network. The customs and protocols advanced in some unspecified time in the future of this time laid the inspiration for the complicated social systems and tribal affiliations that might form Māori society within the centuries to go returned.

The early Māori settlements were characterized by using way of their resilience, adaptability, and deep connection to the land. These businesses established a sturdy feel of identification, cultural practices, and a profound religious connection to their environment. The legacy of their ingenuity, resourcefulness, and harmonious courting with the environment maintains to shape the Māori worldview and enhance the cultural tapestry of New Zealand as a whole.

Chapter 2: Culture And Traditions

Māori manner of existence and traditions are deeply rooted in the values, customs, and spiritual beliefs of the indigenous humans of New Zealand. Central to Māori way of life are tikanga, the same old practices and protocols that manual interactions and behavior, and whakapapa, the interconnectedness of all matters via family tree and ancestry.

Tikanga encompasses a large kind of cultural practices, rituals, and protocols that govern severa components of Māori existence. It offers a framework for know-how and navigating social relationships, land control, aid utilization, and spiritual beliefs. Tikanga is based totally on requirements of apprehend, reciprocity, and the interaction among human beings, the natural environment, and the non secular realm.

Māori tikanga emphasizes the significance of whakapapa, the genealogical connections that hyperlink human beings to their ancestors and to the land. Whakapapa is a idea that extends beyond mere circle of relatives tree, encompassing the spiritual and bodily connections amongst all residing beings and the herbal international. It acknowledges the interconnectedness of past, present, and future generations and the ongoing responsibilities to honor and uphold the legacy of 1's ancestors.

At the coronary coronary heart of whakapapa is the idea of mana, which refers to non-public and collective strength, repute, and authority. Mana is derived from one's whakapapa and is inherited from one's ancestors. It is earned and tested via acts of integrity, management, and upholding the values and obligations related to one's ancestral line.

The idea of whanaungatanga, or kinship, is vital to Māori manner of existence. It acknowledges the interconnectedness of people in the wider circle of relatives and community networks. Whanaungatanga emphasizes the importance of nurturing and preserving strong relationships, fostering harmony, and helping every other. This sense of collective identity and mutual help strengthens the material of Māori society.

Marae, or traditional meeting grounds, hold first rate significance in Māori way of life. These communal areas feature the focal point for gatherings, ceremonies, and cultural practices. Marae are in which tikanga and whakapapa come to life, offering an area for the sharing of memories, songs, dances, and the passing down of cultural facts from one era to the following. Marae moreover provide a platform for crucial discussions, choice-making techniques, and the choice of conflicts inside the network.

The arts, together with carving, weaving, and performing arts, play a vital function in Māori lifestyle. These inventive expressions are imbued with symbolism, cultural narratives, and ancestral connections. Carving, whether or not or not in wooden or stone, showcases complex designs and represents ancestral figures and memories. Weaving, particularly with harakeke (flax), produces sensible and ornamental gadgets that hold cultural significance. Māori appearing arts, such as haka (warfare dance) and waiata (songs), deliver powerful messages and emotions, connecting people to their cultural historical past.

Māori spirituality, known as te ao Māori, includes a belief tool deeply connected to the natural environment and the religious realm. The gods and religious beings play a huge role in Māori cosmology, and their tales and teachings are passed down via oral traditions. Māori spirituality acknowledges the sacredness of the land, rivers, mountains, and forests, thinking about them as residing entities with their own mauri (life strain).

Ceremonies and rituals keep massive significance in Māori subculture, marking vital milestones, which incorporates births, deaths, marriages, and the converting of seasons. These ceremonies frequently incorporate the chanting of karakia (prayers), the sharing of kai (meals), and the providing of waiata and haka. Such rituals make stronger the interconnectedness of humans, the land, and the religious realm, acknowledging the continuing relationships and obligations in the wider network.

Māori manner of lifestyles and traditions hold to thrive in modern-day-day New Zealand, with efforts to revitalize and preserve those rich practices. Through the passing down of knowledge, the celebration of cultural occasions, and the reconnection to ancestral lands, Māori identification and cultural resilience remain sturdy. The popularity of Māori tikanga and whakapapa as vital additives of New Zealand's records fosters a experience of cultural range and appreciation for the contributions of the tangata whenua, the human beings of the land.

Pā and Waka: Māori Fortifications and Canoe Exploration

Pā and waka keep high-quality importance in Māori information, representing crucial additives of Māori manner of existence: fortifications and canoe exploration. These elements finished pivotal roles in shaping the lives and research of the Māori humans in Aotearoa.

Pā, or fortified villages, had been strategically built all through New Zealand. These fortified settlements served as centers of social, cultural, and navy sports activities. Pā have been constructed on extended web sites, which embody hilltops or cliffs, offering herbal protecting blessings. The layout and production of pā severa, reflecting the resources available in clearly considered one of a type regions and the precise desires of the network.

Pā had been normally surrounded with the aid of the use of the use of palisades product of wood stakes, growing a shielding barrier. These palisades served to defend the populace from ability threats, along with rival tribes or outdoor attacks. The entrances to the pā were cautiously guarded and often featured complicated systems of protecting structures, which includes trenches, terraces, and complicated pathways that might make it hard for enemies to penetrate the agreement.

Inside the pā, houses called␣whare have been constructed to offer stable haven for households. These systems were built using a aggregate of natural materials, such as wooden, thatch, and raupō (bulrush) for roofing. Whare have been designed to residence extended families, reinforcing the significance of kinship and communal living within Māori society.

The manufacturing of pā required collective attempt and cooperation in the community. People could come together to smooth the land, acquire materials, and construct the fortifications. These collective endeavors fostered a experience of cohesion, shared obligation, and concord within the network.

Waka, or canoes, executed a essential position in Māori society, allowing exploration, exchange, and the mounted order of latest settlements. Waka had been crafted from large, hollowed-out tree trunks, regularly from the local species of totara or kauri. These strong vessels have been meticulously designed and expertly crafted to stand up to the dreams of extended-distance voyages all through the treacherous waters of the Pacific.

Māori waka have been of various sizes and brands, each serving precise capabilities. Waka taua, or battle canoes, have been built for struggle and will accommodate a big huge form of warriors. Waka tīwai, or sea canoes, had been designed for prolonged voyages and could supply human beings, property, and items. Waka kōpapa, or river canoes, were smaller vessels used for river navigation and inland transport.

The functionality of canoe navigation, known as waka hourua, grow to be specifically evolved among Māori navigators. They used their deep records of celestial navigation, ocean currents, wind styles, and the behavior of marine life to navigate huge stretches of the Pacific Ocean. These intrepid explorers may adopt perilous journeys, often spanning excellent distances, to discover new lands, establish trade networks, and attempting to find property.

Waka exploration done a massive function in shaping the Māori worldview, connecting particular regions, and fostering cultural trade. The voyages allowed for the sharing of knowledge, the exchange of goods, and the installation order of relationships amongst Māori tribes.

The importance of pā and waka extends past their practical capabilities. They constitute the ingenuity, adaptability, and resilience of the Māori human beings. The production of pā displays the resourcefulness and strategic considering the community in times of battle and uncertainty. The voyages undertaken in waka exhibit the navigational prowess, courage, and adventurous spirit of the Māori explorers.

Today, the legacy of pā and waka endures. While pā are not actively used as fortifications, their stays serve as essential archaeological internet web sites and cultural landmarks, reminding us of the rich records and fortitude of the Māori humans. The lifestyle of waka building and navigation remains celebrated and practiced, keeping alive the spirit of exploration, connection, and cultural records.

Pā and waka are emblematic of the power and resilience of the Māori manner of lifestyles, exemplifying the interaction amongst protection and exploration, network and individuality. The enduring presence of these factors in Māori records is a testomony to the profound impact they've got had on shaping the lives and opinions of the Māori people in Aotearoa.

Chapter 3: Life In Prehistoric New Zealand

In prehistoric New Zealand, the Moa hunters were a big agency of folks that thrived in the rich landscapes of the land appeared in recent times as Aotearoa. The Moa hunters, named after the huge flightless birds they hunted, left at the back of a legacy that gives insights into the lives and practices of the early populace of New Zealand.

The Moa hunters belonged to a duration referred to as the Archaic or Initial Period, which lasted from approximately 1300 to 1500 CE. This generation changed into characterised through the usage of a hunter-gatherer manner of existence, with the Moa hunters relying on the natural property available to them for sustenance and survival.

The primary attention of the Moa hunters' subsistence modified into the looking of the Moa, a set of big, flightless birds endemic to New Zealand. These birds, belonging to the ratite circle of relatives, ranged in period from small to large, with the largest species attaining heights of over three meters. The Moa supplied a treasured source of meat, feathers, and bones, which have been accomplished for numerous functions in the network.

To hunt the Moa, the Moa hunters hired pretty some of techniques and techniques. They may track and stalk the birds, using their expertise of the panorama and the conduct of the Moa to their gain. The Moa hunters were expert with their guns, which blanketed spears and wood golf equipment. They may additionally cautiously method the Moa and deliver unique moves to ensure a a success kill.

The Moa hunters' looking practices were not limited to the Moa on my own. They moreover hunted one-of-a-type local fauna, consisting of seals, sea lions, and severa chook species. Additionally, they engaged in accumulating sports activities, collecting a diverse sort of plant belongings, which encompass berries, roots, and leaves.

The life-style of the Moa hunters became surprisingly cellular, with small family corporations or prolonged kinship networks moving at some point of the land looking for resources. They lived in short campsites, regularly close to assets of freshwater or meals. These campsites offer treasured archaeological proof of the Moa hunters' sports activities activities, revealing the device, artifacts, and remnants of their each day lives.

The Moa hunters had a deep connection to the land and its property. They possessed an intimate facts of their environment, data the seasonal styles, the migration of animals, and the supply of plant resources. This records have come to be exceeded down through generations, contributing to their adaptability and survival inside the difficult landscapes of prehistoric New Zealand.

Archaeological evidence indicates that the Moa hunters had a rich cloth way of existence. They crafted gear from various materials, which include stone, bone, and timber. Stone equipment, consisting of adzes, have been crucial for lowering, carving, and shaping wooden and specific substances. Bone gadget, together with fish hooks and needles, had been used for fishing, weaving, and particular duties. These artifacts offer insights into the skills and craftsmanship of the Moa hunters, demonstrating their resourcefulness and ingenuity.

The Moa hunters' manner of life began to change with the advent of latest waves of settlers, referred to as the Classic Māori length, across the 14th century. These inexperienced people added with them new technology, inclusive of the cultivation of vegetation like kūmara (sweet potato), and new techniques of fishing and food manufacturing. This length marked a large shift in Māori society, leading to the repute quo of massive, more eternal settlements and the improvement of greater complex social systems.

The legacy of the Moa hunters is an critical part of New Zealand's cultural historical past. Their manner of existence, looking practices, and understanding of the land contributed to the foundation of Māori life-style and traditions that keep to shape the identification of the Māori human beings these days. The Moa hunters' resilience, adaptability, and resourcefulness are a testament to the human capability to thrive in numerous environments and to the iconic connection amongst human beings and their herbal environment.

Waitaha and Kāti Mamoe: Predecessors to Ngāi Tahu

Before the upward push of Ngāi Tahu as a dominant Māori iwi (tribe) in the South Island of New Zealand, the land became inhabited via certainly one of a kind large tribal groups: Waitaha and Kāti Mamoe. These corporations, with their very very own specific histories and cultural practices, carried out critical roles in shaping the panorama and putting the degree for the advent of Ngāi Tahu.

Waitaha, believed to be the earliest populace of the South Island, hooked up themselves alongside the coast and inland regions. The origins of Waitaha are despite the fact that the task of ongoing studies and debate amongst historians and college students. It is thought that they arrived in

Aotearoa from Polynesia, likely via voyages in some unspecified time in the future of the Pacific Ocean, in a period predating the 14th century.

Waitaha advanced their non-public brilliant traditions, social systems, and customs within the direction in their time inside the South Island. They had a near connection to the land and were professional in the usage of the herbal sources available to them for sustenance and cultural expression. Their presence contributed to the shaping of the bodily and cultural landscape of the region.

Kāti Mamoe, some other big tribal institution within the South Island, emerged after the advent of Waitaha. Their actual origins and the times in their migration aren't as nicely-documented as the ones of Waitaha. Kāti Mamoe is thought to have originated from a combination of Polynesian and earlier indigenous populations, blending with modern corporations in the South Island.

Kāti Mamoe set up settlements and advanced their personal precise cultural practices, notable from every Waitaha and later arrivals which encompass Ngāi Tahu. They had their very very very own social structures, manage systems, and relationships with the land. Kāti Mamoe agencies occupied numerous elements of the South Island, which encompass the coastal areas and the indoors valleys.

The interactions and relationships amongst Waitaha, Kāti Mamoe, and Ngāi Tahu have been complicated and varied. Over time, Ngāi Tahu, a tribe from the North Island, migrated to the South Island, step by step maintaining their have an impact on and putting in their presence inside the place. This gadget worried a mixture of non violent integration, intermarriage, and, at times, war the diverse awesome tribal groups.

The arrival of Ngāi Tahu marked a large turning detail inside the history of the South Island, as they in the long run have emerge as the dominant pressure inside the place. However, it's miles critical to understand and well known the massive contributions and legacies of Waitaha and Kāti Mamoe. Their histories, cultural practices, and connection to the land preserve to shape the identification and history of the South Island, interwoven with the narratives of Ngāi Tahu and next waves of migration and agreement.

Today, the descendants of Waitaha and Kāti Mamoe, along Ngāi Tahu, shape part of the wider Māori network inside the South Island. Efforts to hold and revitalize their specific cultural traditions and historic narratives make a contribution to the rich tapestry of Māori manner of lifestyles in New Zealand. The legacies of Waitaha and Kāti Mamoe are a testament to the resilience, adaptability, and enduring presence of numerous Māori tribal corporations inside the land of Aotearoa.

Ngāti Toa and Te Rauparaha: Warriors and Migration

Ngāti Toa and their renowned chief Te Rauparaha maintain a fantastic region in the data of New Zealand. As a effective tribal employer, Ngāti Toa finished a important function in shaping the political panorama and cultural fabric of the u . S . A ., specially inside the applicable and lower North Island.

Ngāti Toa lines its lineage decrease back to the ancestral determine Toarangatira, a outstanding rangatira (chief) and chief of the iwi (tribe). The origins of Ngāti Toa may be associated with the migration of their ancestors from their ancestral location of birth within the Taranaki location to the Kapiti Coast and the wider Wellington region.

Te Rauparaha, a renowned and influential leader, emerged as a crucial determine in Ngāti Toa's statistics. Known for his military prowess, strategic vision, and political acumen, Te Rauparaha finished a pivotal role within the boom of Ngāti Toa's territory and effect.

Te Rauparaha's manipulate is specifically related to the duration of intertribal conflicts and upheavals called the Musket Wars, which occurred inside the early nineteenth century. During this time, Te Rauparaha skillfully implemented firearms acquired via early European touch to enhance Ngāti Toa's military energy and growth their territorial control.

One of the maximum outstanding events related to Ngāti Toa and Te Rauparaha is the migration known as the Te Heke Tōtara, or the Great Migration. Faced with the encroachment of rival tribes and the impact of European colonization, Ngāti Toa launched into a chain of migrations, in are trying to find of latest territories and possibilities for his or her human beings.

The Te Heke Tōtara migration saw Ngāti Toa traverse the North Island, venturing thru one in all a type regions and encountering numerous worrying situations alongside the way. Their trips took them from the Kapiti Coast to areas which incorporates Manawatū, Rangitīkei, and sooner or later to the Whanganui location. This migration changed right into a testomony to the resilience, adaptability, and determination of Ngāti Toa as they sought to solid their human beings's future.

The migration of Ngāti Toa and Te Rauparaha had sizable results for the regions they encountered. It caused each alliances and conflicts with one-of-a-kind tribes as they sought to set up new settlements and assert their authority. The impact of those interactions reverberated throughout the North Island, shaping the political dynamics and cultural panorama of the areas they traversed.

Te Rauparaha's management prolonged beyond navy endeavors. He have turn out to be moreover recognized as a poet and composer of waiata (songs), leaving a legacy of poetic expressions that stay celebrated and done in recent times. His composition "Ka Mate," finished in haka (warfare dance), is one of the maximum famous and extensively completed waiata in Māori way of life.

The have an effect on of Ngāti Toa and Te Rauparaha extended beyond their immediately surroundings. Their interactions with early European settlers, mainly inside the course of the duration of colonization, executed a giant feature in shaping the information of New Zealand. The signing of the Treaty of Waitangi in 1840 noticed Ngāti Toa and Te Rauparaha have interaction with European government and navigate the complexities of colonial governance.

Today, Ngāti Toa stays an critical Māori iwi, preserving its cultural traditions, connections to the land, and contributions to the wider Māori network. The legacy of Te Rauparaha and the migrations of Ngāti Toa feature a reminder of the staying energy, strength, and cultural history of the people who've called Aotearoa home for generations.

Chapter 4: Conflict And Change

Hongi Hika, a prominent Māori chief and warrior, played a huge function in the information of New Zealand at some stage inside the early 19th century. His movements and manage within the Northern War, additionally called the Musket Wars, delivered about substantial struggle and exchange, shaping the political panorama of the North Island.

Hongi Hika come to be a Ngāpuhi leader, belonging to the influential iwi (tribe) primarily based in the Northland vicinity of New Zealand. Known for his navy prowess and ambition, Hongi Hika sought to growth Ngāpuhi's have an impact on and strong property and mana (fame) for his humans.

The Northern War have become a length of immoderate intertribal conflicts and struggle that befell amongst diverse Māori tribes from the late 18th century to the early nineteenth century. This duration turn out to be marked with the useful resource of multiplied tribal hostilities, pushed in element by way of way of way of the introduction of muskets acquired via early European touch.

Hongi Hika observed the ability military benefit of acquiring European firearms and ammunition, and he embarked on a undertaking to normal the ones weapons thru exchange and particular technique. With the purchase of muskets, Hongi Hika considerably improved the navy capabilities of Ngāpuhi and sought to leverage this gain in his goals for territorial growth.

Under Hongi Hika's leadership, Ngāpuhi engaged in a chain of campaigns and battles closer to rival tribes, utilising the newfound firepower to devastating effect. The conflicts within the route of this time had been characterized with the resource of the use of strategic navy techniques, sieges, and the pursuit of territorial manipulate.

Hongi Hika's maximum well-known advertising and advertising advertising campaign befell in 1821, even as he led an super battle birthday celebration southward, focused on tribes in the Waikato region. This day journey led to great losses and casualties, however it moreover solidified Ngāpuhi's popularity as a powerful strain to be reckoned with.

The effect of the Northern War extended past the immediately conflicts. The full-size use of muskets converted the man or woman of warfare in New Zealand, intensifying hostilities and increasing the dimensions of the battles. The creation of firearms altered the stableness of strength among tribes, with those owning muskets gaining a huge benefit over individuals who did not.

The Northern War brought about profound modifications in the political and social dynamics of the North Island. The conflicts resulted in the redistribution of territories and the realignment of tribal alliances. Tribes which have been as soon as dominant located themselves displaced, on the same time as others, which includes Ngāpuhi, extended their affect and authority.

While the Northern War turn out to be characterised with the useful useful resource of war and violence, it also performed a feature in shaping subsequent efforts in the direction of peace and reconciliation. The devastating effect of the conflicts precipitated a few Māori leaders to are searching out options to battle and to discover diplomatic channels for resolving disputes. This ultimately added about the signing of the Treaty of Waitangi in 1840, which hooked up a foundation for the relationship among Māori and the British Crown.

Hongi Hika's impact prolonged beyond his military exploits. He was additionally stated for his intelligence, global own family individuals, and cultural exchanges with Europeans. He engaged in interactions with early European traffic, together with Samuel Marsden and Thomas Kendall, fostering relationships and exploring possibilities for change and cultural change.

The legacy of Hongi Hika and the Northern War is complex and multifaceted. While the conflicts added about big devastation and loss, similarly they done a detail in shaping the subsequent facts of New Zealand. The Northern War marked a period of trade, realignment, and reevaluation of strength dynamics amongst Māori tribes. It serves as a reminder of the complexities of colonial encounters and the ongoing efforts in the direction of reconciliation and nation-building in New Zealand.

The Treaty of Waitangi: A Founding Document

The Treaty of Waitangi is a pivotal file in the statistics of New Zealand, representing a big 2nd of interplay and settlement among Māori and the British Crown. Signed on February 6, 1840, the Treaty has due to the truth that end up a cornerstone of New Zealand's constitutional framework and a symbol of the relationship the diverse Māori people and the authorities.

The origins of the Treaty may be traced decrease lower back to worries raised through each Māori and British settlers concerning the need for governance, land rights, and the protection of person pursuits. British officers diagnosed the importance of organising a framework for governance and securing British authority in the wake of growing European immigration and settlement.

The Treaty end up drafted through a sequence of discussions and negotiations between representatives of the British Crown, led with the useful resource of William Hobson, and various Māori chiefs from particular iwi (tribes) all through Aotearoa. The primary Māori signatories of the Treaty had been recommended to build up at numerous places sooner or later of the u . S ., which encompass Waitangi, Hokianga, and Manukau.

The Treaty includes 3 maximum vital files: the English version, the Māori model (Te Tiriti o Waitangi), and the Māori translation of the English version. While the English and Māori versions deliver similar thoughts, there are nuanced versions the various texts, essential to ongoing discussions and debates regarding their interpretation.

The Treaty of Waitangi addresses several key elements, collectively with the popularity of Māori rangatiratanga (chieftainship), the switch of sovereignty to the British Crown, the safety of Māori land and resources, and the extension of British citizenship to Māori. The Māori model emphasizes the retention of Māori authority and the guarantee of te tino rangatiratanga (complete manage and authority) over their lands, sources, and taonga (treasures).

The signing of the Treaty have become not a unified event, and the understandings and intentions of the Māori signatories numerous. Some chiefs signed with the expectancy that it would steady protection for his or her lands and guarantee their persevered autonomy, on the identical time as others sought to installation a partnership with the British Crown primarily based completely mostly on mutual recognize and cooperation.

The Treaty of Waitangi, first of all visible as a massive step in the direction of establishing a framework for governance and shielding Māori hobbies, confronted demanding conditions in its implementation. The British interpretation and alertness of the Treaty regularly diverged from the expectancies of Māori signatories. Issues including land confiscations, breaches of the Treaty's ideas, and cultural assimilation guidelines brought on discontent amongst Māori companies and ongoing struggles for justice and redress.

The significance of the Treaty of Waitangi has advanced over time. Initially, it served as a prison foundation for British governance in New Zealand. However, within the latter half of of of the 20th century, the Treaty received accelerated recognition as a founding document of the kingdom, with the requirements of partnership, participation, and protection turning into essential to New Zealand's constitutional framework.

Efforts to honor the Treaty and cope with historical injustices had been ongoing. The fame quo of the Waitangi Tribunal in 1975 supplied a mechanism for Māori to searching out redress for Treaty breaches, together with land confiscations and breaches of the Treaty's ideas. The tribunal's findings and tips have performed a crucial position in selling reconciliation, acknowledging beyond wrongs, and fostering a higher records of the Treaty's purpose and implications.

The Treaty of Waitangi continues to be a residing file, shaping the relationship a number of the Māori people and the authorities of New Zealand. It serves as a platform for ongoing communicate, negotiation, and partnership amongst Māori and non-Māori businesses, striving within the course of a extra equitable and inclusive society. The Treaty's standards are included into severa elements of New Zealand's crook tool, authorities guidelines, and cultural practices, emphasizing the continuing dedication to honoring the Treaty's spirit and motive.

Colonial New Zealand: British Settlement and Governance

Colonial New Zealand marks a huge length within the facts of the u . S ., characterised by means of British agreement, governance, and the impact of European colonization. The arrival of British settlers delivered about profound modifications to the social, political, and cultural panorama of Aotearoa.

British hobby in New Zealand as a ability colony grew at some diploma in the past due 18th and early nineteenth centuries. Explorers which incorporates James Cook and sealers like Captain George Vancouver contributed to the European know-how of the land and its belongings. These early encounters set the volume for future British involvement in New Zealand.

The first prepared British settlement in New Zealand occurred in 1814 at the same time as Samuel Marsden set up a task in the Bay of Islands. The task aimed to spread Christianity and establish non violent relationships with Māori businesses. Marsden's challenge marked the start of a greater good sized wave of British migration and colonization.

The signing of the Treaty of Waitangi in 1840 laid the idea for British governance in New Zealand. The British Crown sought to establish its authority, hold law and order, and shield the hobbies of British settlers on the equal time as acknowledging the rights and pastimes of Māori. The Treaty furnished a criminal framework for the relationship among Māori and the British authorities.

As British settlers arrived in big numbers, organized colonial settlements had been hooked up at some stage in the u . S . A .. Wellington, Auckland, and Christchurch have emerge as essential centers of management, alternate, and manner of life. The settlers brought with them their very non-public customs, institutions, and era, shaping the improvement of New Zealand's colonial society.

The British government done a terrific function inside the governance of colonial New Zealand. Initially, New Zealand turned into administered as part of the colony of New South Wales. However, in 1841, it have emerge as a separate colony with its very private governor and legislative council. The British-appointed governors had the authority to make selections concerning land possession, governance, and the implementation of colonial hints.

The colonial government carried out severa policies and practices that impacted each Māori and non-Māori communities. The New Zealand Constitution Act of 1852 set up a consultant authorities, offering a framework for democratic governance. However, it's far essential to phrase that Māori example grow to be constrained at some stage in this time, leading to disparities in political power and choice-making.

One of the defining talents of colonial New Zealand changed into the approach of land acquisition and settlement. The British government finished pointers that facilitated the acquisition of land from

Māori, regularly through the debatable mechanism of the land purchase gadget. This system led to top notch land loss for Māori and taken approximately ongoing grievances and disputes.

The discovery of gold in the mid-nineteenth century added about a fast inflow of settlers, further accelerating the boom and development of colonial New Zealand. The gold rushes attracted people from spherical the world, contributing to a diverse population and cultural exchange.

Over time, the colonial government done measures aimed closer to assimilating Māori into British society. These guidelines included the established order of schools, the imposition of European-fashion land tenure systems, and tries to suppress Māori cultural practices. Such policies had a profound effect on Māori communities, contributing to the erosion of conventional practices and social systems.

The colonial period in New Zealand come to be now not with out conflicts and tensions. The New Zealand Wars, fought among 1845 and 1872, had been a chain of armed conflicts among Māori and the British authorities and its settler allies. These wars have been driven through manner of a range of things, inclusive of land disputes, cultural clashes, and resistance to colonial authority.

The legacy of colonial New Zealand is complicated and multifaceted. The length added approximately big societal modifications, the hooked up order of institutions, and the advent of recent technology and practices. It moreover resulted in the marginalization and dispossession of Māori corporations, major to ongoing efforts for redress, reconciliation, and the recognition of the rights and cultural background of the tangata whenua, the humans of the land.

The colonial technology paperwork an essential part of New Zealand's statistics, contributing to the country's cultural range and shaping the inspiration upon which the cutting-edge-day u . S . Has been constructed. It serves as a reminder of the complexities and traumatic conditions inherent within the techniques of colonization and the persevering with pursuit of social justice and equality.

Chapter 5: The New Zealand Wars

The New Zealand Wars, spanning from 1845 to 1872, had been a sequence of armed conflicts amongst Māori tribes and the British government, in addition to colonial settlers. These conflicts emerged due to land disputes, cultural clashes, and resistance to colonial authority, shaping the route of New Zealand's facts.

The wars have been driven through a complicated interplay of political, monetary, and cultural factors. Land acquisition and settler boom achieved a outstanding characteristic, because the developing numbers of European immigrants positioned pressure on Māori land and assets. This brought about conflicts bobbing up from conflicting land claims, the implementation of the land buy device, and the erosion of Māori land possession.

The preliminary conflicts within the 1840s, called the Flagstaff War or the Northern War, occurred within the Northland location. These conflicts worried clashes amongst Māori tribes, extensively Ngāpuhi, and British forces. The British sought to assert their authority and protect British settlers, while Māori resisted encroachments on their lands and sovereignty.

The Taranaki location modified into a focus of struggle within the 1860s, with the First Taranaki War (1860-1861) and the Second Taranaki War (1863-1866) being large episodes. These conflicts focused round land confiscations, damaged guarantees, and the reputation quo of a British army presence in the location. Māori resistance, led with the resource of figures which encompass Wiremu Kingi Te Rangitāke and Titokowaru, ended in extended engagements and guerrilla battle strategies.

The Waikato War (1863-1864) emerge as every other fundamental war all through this era. It arose from tensions surrounding the land confiscation coverage, the enlargement of European settlements, and the selection of the British government to mention manage over the Waikato place. Māori forces, led with the useful resource of leaders including Rewi Maniapoto and Wiremu Tamihana, resisted British navy campaigns, ensuing in fierce battles and the eventual career of the vicinity.

The conflicts in the valuable North Island, consisting of the Battle of Orakau and the siege of Pāterangi, validated the resilience and resolution of Māori forces in the face of overwhelming British military strength. Māori strategies, consisting of the improvement of properly-fortified pā (fortifications) and the powerful use of trench conflict, showcased their army talents.

The conflicts in the Bay of Plenty and the East Coast, which encompass the campaigns led thru the usage of Māori leader Te Kooti and the resistance at Gate Pā and Te Ranga, similarly exemplified the complexities and intensities of the New Zealand Wars. These engagements had been characterised with the useful aid of each traditional and guerilla battle techniques, highlighting the adaptability and strategic thinking of Māori fighters.

The consequences of the New Zealand Wars have been far-task. They resulted in giant loss of existence, displacement of groups, and the confiscation of Māori land. The wars additionally had profound social, cultural, and political influences, shaping the connection among Māori and the Crown, and the improvement of New Zealand as a state.

Following the realization of the wars, the Crown pursued a coverage of land confiscation, often focused on the ones deemed to be "rebels" or resisting British authority. These confiscations in addition compounded the lack of Māori land and contributed to ongoing grievances and injustices.

The New Zealand Wars also had an extended-lasting effect on cultural practices and relationships among Māori and non-Māori groups. The conflicts disrupted traditional strategies of life, introduced approximately the displacement of groups, and resulted in the loss of ancestral lands. The scars of those conflicts stay felt these days, with efforts for reconciliation, redress, and the popularity of the rights and cultural records of Māori corporations.

It is essential to observe that the New Zealand Wars have been complex and concerned more than one events. Māori have been not a homogeneous institution, and the conflicts determined each alliances and divisions amongst Māori tribes. Additionally, no longer all Māori tribes participated inside the wars, and some sought non violent resolutions to the land disputes and conflicts.

The New Zealand Wars live a topic of ongoing studies, reflected image, and talk in New Zealand. Efforts to widely known the injustices of the past, promote know-how, and foster a greater inclusive society maintain to form the u . S .'s collective memory and aspirations for a shared destiny.

Gold Rush and Immigration: Seeking Wealth and Opportunity

The discovery of gold in New Zealand inside the mid-19th century sparked a first rate influx of people from spherical the arena, as humans sought to capitalize at the potential wealth and opportunities that lay in the goldfields. The gold rushes added approximately transformative social, financial, and cultural adjustments, leaving a protracted-lasting impact at the improvement of the usa of the usa.

The first important gold rush took place in 1852 inside the Coromandel region, attracting hopeful prospectors from nearby areas and further afield. This initial rush end up accompanied with the beneficial resource of subsequent discoveries in numerous components of the us, along side Otago, West Coast, and Thames. Each goldfield had its very very own unique developments and attracted numerous organizations of human beings.

Gold rushes added collectively humans from diverse backgrounds and nationalities. European settlers, predominantly from Britain, flocked to the goldfields attempting to find fortune. However, the gold rushes additionally attracted miners and entrepreneurs from Australia, California, China, and awesome elements of the sector. This inflow of humans contributed to the multicultural material of New Zealand society.

The gold rushes had a profound impact at the economic device of New Zealand. They stimulated economic boom, created employment possibilities, and fueled the improvement of infrastructure and offerings inside the regions affected by the rushes. Towns and settlements suddenly grew as miners and their households established houses, corporations, and assisting services.

The goldfields were tough and demanding environments. Miners faced harsh conditions, jogging lengthy hours in bodily stressful and frequently risky situations. They used pretty a few techniques, at the side of panning, sluicing, and hydraulic mining, to extract gold from the rivers, streams, and alluvial deposits.

The attraction of gold drew people from all walks of life. Miners ranged from professional specialists to green humans looking for a glowing start. The goldfields furnished opportunities for social mobility and economic improvement, as a hit miners must gather wealth and installation themselves within the growing society.

Chinese miners executed a big characteristic within the New Zealand gold rushes. Large numbers of Chinese migrants arrived looking for gold, in particular in a few unspecified time inside the future of the Otago and West Coast rushes. They delivered with them their private mining strategies and cultural practices, contributing to the multicultural landscape of the goldfields.

The gold rushes also brought approximately societal and cultural changes. The rapid inflow of humans and the established order of severa groups brought about the development of latest social systems, establishments, and norms. Law and order needed to be mounted, and governing our our bodies have been fashioned to maintain order and administer justice inside the goldfields.

The gold rushes had an extended-lasting effect on the areas in which they happened. Some cities that sprang up in some unspecified time within the future of the rushes, which includes Queenstown and Arrowtown in Otago, keep to thrive in recent times, their increase and prosperity rooted within the legacy of the gold rushes. The architectural background, historic sites, and cultural affects associated with the goldfields feature a reminder of this transformative technology.

While the gold rushes brought financial possibilities, moreover they had environmental effects. The massive mining sports, which includes using chemical compounds together with mercury, precipitated tremendous adjustments to the panorama and the ecosystems of the affected areas. The environmental affects of the gold rushes stay studied and managed these days.

As the with out problem on hand gold became depleted, the gold rushes step by step declined. However, the legacies of the rushes and the multicultural influences they brought persist. The gold rushes continue to be an critical bankruptcy in New Zealand's statistics, representing a length of pleasure, ambition, and the pursuit of wealth and possibility. The testimonies of the miners, their struggles, and successes hold to capture the creativeness and contribute to the rich tapestry of New Zealand's cultural background.

Dunedin and the Otago Settlement: A Scottish Influence

The town of Dunedin, located in the Otago place of New Zealand, holds a rich records deeply intertwined with Scottish influences. The installed order of the Otago Settlement in the mid-nineteenth century introduced a huge Scottish presence to the region, shaping its manner of lifestyles, shape, schooling, and identity.

The Otago Settlement end up based by using manner of the Free Church of Scotland as a deliberate Presbyterian settlement. Seeking to create a haven for his or her spiritual network, the Free Church sent out a fixed of settlers led via Captain William Cargill and Reverend Thomas Burns. The first settlers arrived in 1848, and the rules of Dunedin, known as the "Edinburgh of the South," were laid.

The Scottish have an effect on on Dunedin and the broader Otago location grow to be profound. Many of the early settlers have been of Scottish descent, and that they brought with them their traditions, customs, and values. This protected the upkeep of the Presbyterian faith, the Gaelic language, and a sturdy experience of community.

Dunedin's town planning and shape mirror its Scottish records. The town's avenue layout, with its grid sample and amazing octagon-formed town middle, mirrors the layout of Scottish towns collectively with Edinburgh. The use of nearby bluestone in the arrival of homes, on the aspect of the presence of Victorian and Edwardian architectural styles, provides to the city's particular character.

Education performed a crucial function inside the Scottish have an effect on on Dunedin. The settlers recognized the importance of schooling and hooked up the University of Otago in 1869, making it New Zealand's first university. The university's Scottish roots are obvious in its educational traditions and the Scottish-inspired Knox College, clearly one among its residential schools.

The Scottish have an impact on prolonged beyond training to different cultural additives of Dunedin. Scottish societies, Caledonian gatherings, and Highland Games have grow to be crucial network activities, offering a location for the celebration and protection of Scottish historical past. Bagpipe bands, Scottish dancing, and traditional Scottish song and clothing have come to be cherished factors of Dunedin's cultural fabric.

Economically, the Otago gold rushes in the mid-nineteenth century further fueled the boom and improvement of Dunedin. The influx of wealth from gold mining, in conjunction with the status quo of industries which embody agriculture, sheep farming, and brewing, contributed to Dunedin's prosperity and strengthened its reputation as a prominent center of commerce and exchange.

The Scottish have an impact on on Dunedin can also be seen in its vicinity names. Many places inside the area go through Scottish names, reflecting the settlers' connections to their homeland. Names which includes Edinburgh, Glasgow, and Balclutha pay homage to the Scottish origins of the settlers and feature a reminder in their enduring legacy.

As time passed, the cultural landscape of Dunedin developed, and the city have turn out to be more various. However, the Scottish have an impact on remains a huge a part of the metropolis's identification, cherished and celebrated via each residents and site visitors alike. It serves as a testomony to the long-lasting connections among New Zealand and Scotland and the contributions made thru the usage of Scottish settlers to the improvement of Dunedin and the Otago area.

Today, Dunedin continues to embody its Scottish historical beyond through severa cultural sports, gala's, and agencies. The Dunedin Scottish Festival, held every 12 months, showcases Scottish tune, dance, and traditions. Scottish societies and pipe bands make a contribution to the vibrancy of the metropolis's cultural scene, maintaining the Scottish have an impact on alive and fostering a revel in of pride in Dunedin's particular statistics.

The Scottish have an effect on on Dunedin and the Otago Settlement is a testomony to the iconic impact of early Scottish settlers and their contributions to the development of New Zealand. Their ancient beyond, traditions, and values have formed Dunedin right into a metropolis that embraces its Scottish roots at the same time as embracing multiculturalism and the form of its contemporary populace.

Chapter 6: The Canterbury Plains Anglican Faith And Agriculture

The Canterbury Plains, placed at the eastern coast of New Zealand's South Island, have a rich records deeply associated with the Anglican faith and agricultural development. The settlement of the Canterbury vicinity have emerge as pushed by manner of way of a preference to installation a planned Anglican community and growth the fertile land for farming and agriculture.

The origins of the Canterbury settlement may be traced back to the 1840s while the Canterbury Association, led via John Robert Godley, sought to create a contemporary-day English-style colony in New Zealand. The founders expected a society based totally absolutely at the standards of the Church of England and a flourishing agricultural financial gadget.

The Anglican Church played a number one feature inside the status quo and improvement of the Canterbury region. The Canterbury Association sought to create a version Anglican settlement, in which the Anglican faith and its requirements may form the social and cultural fabric of the network. The iconic ChristChurch Cathedral, located inside the coronary heart of Christchurch, have grow to be a symbol of the Anglican have an effect on inside the location.

The founding of Christ's College in 1850 similarly emphasized the significance of education and the Anglican ethos within the Canterbury settlement. The university supplied a basis for educational and religious development, instilling Anglican values and traditions within the younger minds of the vicinity.

The Canterbury Plains provided fertile land, first-rate for agricultural endeavors.

The early settlers recognized the rural potential of the location and launched into clearing the land, establishing farms, and growing a thriving agricultural enterprise agency. The fertility of the Canterbury Plains, coupled with the modern farming practices added with the useful resource of the settlers, enabled the vicinity to turn out to be a full-size agricultural powerhouse.

The advent of recent farming techniques and the cultivation of plant life together with wheat, barley, and oats allowed the Canterbury Plains to grow to be called the "Granary of New Zealand." The success of the agricultural industry contributed to the financial increase and prosperity of the region, attracting further waves of settlers seeking out opportunities in farming and related industries.

The development of infrastructure, which include roads, railways, and irrigation structures, in addition facilitated agricultural growth inside the Canterbury location. The advent of the Main South Line railway, connecting Christchurch with the rest of the South Island, finished a vital function in transporting agricultural produce to markets and facilitating exchange.

The Anglican Church's have an impact on prolonged past religious and educational spheres. It also completed a characteristic in the social and cultural lifestyles of the Canterbury region. The Anglican Church acted as a focus for community gatherings, social activities, and charitable sports. The church's presence and help supplied a sense of balance, community, and ethical guidance to the settlers.

The Anglican affect at the Canterbury Plains remains obvious today. ChristChurch Cathedral, however the damage suffered in the 2011 earthquake, remains an iconic photograph of the place. The Anglican religion keeps to shape the non secular landscape, with numerous Anglican churches scattered all through the Canterbury vicinity, imparting religious steerage and assist to the network.

Agriculture remains a crucial issue of the Canterbury Plains' economic system. The place is famend for its severa agricultural sports, along with dairy farming, sheep farming, horticulture, and viticulture. The fertile soils, favorable weather, and modern farming practices keep to make contributions to the vicinity's agricultural success.

The Canterbury Plains' statistics as an Anglican agreement and its agricultural legacy are important components of the vicinity's identification. The connection amongst religion and farming original the social, cultural, and monetary improvement of the Canterbury area.

Today, the Canterbury Plains stand as a testomony to the vision, resilience, and hard work of the early settlers who hooked up a flourishing Anglican community and converted the land proper right right into a thriving agricultural heartland.

Early European Explorers: Mapping New Zealand's Wilderness

The exploration of New Zealand with the aid of manner of using early European navigators and explorers marked the start of European contact with the islands. These intrepid explorers ventured into the unknown, mapping the wasteland, and revealing the existence of this some distance off land to the rest of the arena.

One of the primary European explorers to encounter New Zealand grow to be the Dutch navigator Abel Tasman. In 1642, Tasman sighted the northwest coast of the

South Island, which he named Staten Landt. He then sailed along the western coast of the North Island, charting the coastline and making word of the Māori populace he encountered.

Tasman's encounters with Māori had been not continually peaceful, and a battle of words with Māori warriors caused severa deaths on every elements. These encounters left a cautious have an effect on on next European explorers and inspired their technique to appealing with the indigenous population.

It wasn't till the past due 18th century that further European explorers, specially the ones from Britain, commenced out to discover and chart New Zealand in greater detail. Captain James Cook, on his first voyage to the Pacific in 1769, arrived in New Zealand and spent numerous months mapping the coastline and making one in all a kind observations of the land, flowers, fauna, and Māori lifestyle.

Cook's mapping of New Zealand's shoreline became a extremely good contribution to the world's information of the islands' geography. His meticulous charting and observations provided a basis for destiny explorers, navigators, and cartographers.

During subsequent voyages, Cook persevered to discover and map New Zealand, refining the accuracy of in advance maps and documenting numerous capabilities of the land. Cook's observations and writings approximately New Zealand's natural property, collectively with wood, seals, whales, and flora, sparked interest amongst European worldwide places.

Other explorers and navigators accompanied in Cook's footsteps, constructing upon his art work and increasing information of New Zealand. These protected first rate figures such as Jean-François-Marie de Surville, who arrived in 1769, and Jules Dumont d'Urville, who done huge clinical research and mapping sooner or later of his visits inside the early nineteenth century.

The mapping of New Zealand's barren area with the useful resource of those early European explorers unveiled the united states's diverse topography, which consist of its mountain ranges, rivers, lakes, and coastal features. Their observations and maps helped set up a extra accurate understanding of New Zealand's geography and assisted in next agreement and useful resource exploration.

European exploration and mapping of New Zealand have been no longer without annoying conditions. The rugged terrain, dense forests, and unpredictable climate provided formidable barriers to navigation and mapping. Explorers frequently confronted troubles in appropriately charting the complicated coastlines and making experience of the complex network of fjords, bays, and harbors.

The interactions amongst European explorers and Māori numerous appreciably. While a few encounters have been marked by way of manner of peaceful interactions, cultural exchange, and shared knowledge, others had been characterized thru way of misunderstandings, war, and violence. The explorers' opinions with Māori inspired subsequent European perceptions of the indigenous population and impacted the course of European settlement and engagement with Māori groups.

The mapping and exploration of New Zealand via early European explorers unfolded possibilities for similarly contact, exchange, and finally colonization. Their efforts now not most effective provided valuable geographical data however moreover ignited hobby within the islands and laid the muse for next waves of European migration and settlement.

The contributions of these early European explorers in mapping New Zealand's barren place had been huge in growing knowledge of the location, shaping perceptions of the land and its human beings, and paving the manner for further exploration and engagement. Their maps and information remain valuable historic files, offering perception into the early interactions between Europeans and the indigenous population of New Zealand.

Chapter 7: The Southern Alps And Fiordland

The Southern Alps and Fiordland areas of New Zealand boast some of the maximum awe-inspiring and majestic landscapes in the u . S .. These natural wonders have captivated the creativeness of web page site visitors and locals alike, showcasing the raw splendor and rugged grandeur of New Zealand's barren region.

The Southern Alps, extending for about 500 kilometers down the spine of the South Island, are a remarkable mountain variety that dominates the landscape. Mount Cook, additionally referred to as Aoraki, is the very first-rate top in New Zealand, reputation at an impressive three,724 meters. The Southern Alps are domestic to severa special towering peaks, glaciers, and alpine landscapes, growing a dramatic and breathtaking landscape.

Glaciers are amazing abilities of the Southern Alps, with the most famous being the Franz Josef Glacier and the Fox Glacier. These massive rivers of ice drift from the excessive mountain peaks down into lush rainforests, a phenomenon that is unusual and unique globally. The dynamic nature of those glaciers creates a continuously changing and evolving landscape.

The Southern Alps also are famend for his or her lovely alpine lakes. Lake Tekapo, with its charming turquoise waters, is a well-known destination for visitors searching for tranquility and natural beauty. Lake Pukaki, seemed for its colourful blue hue, gives breathtaking perspectives of the surrounding mountains, including Mount Cook.

Fiordland, positioned in the southwestern corner of the South Island, is a vicinity of elegant beauty and untouched barren region. It is characterised with the resource of the usage of its deep, slender fiords, carved via manner of historical glacial interest. Milford Sound and Doubtful Sound, of the most well-known fiords in Fiordland, trap web page traffic from spherical the area with their sheer cliffs, cascading waterfalls, and pristine landscapes.

Milford Sound, frequently referred to as the "Eighth Wonder of the World," is an area of awe-inspiring herbal beauty. The towering Mitre Peak, growing dramatically from the waters, creates an iconic photograph synonymous with Fiordland's beauty. The fiord is likewise home to an abundance of herbal world, together with seals, dolphins, and penguins, which includes to its ecological importance.

Doubtful Sound, a more secluded and far off fiord, gives a revel in of tranquility and solitude. Its untouched barren vicinity and dense rainforests provide a sanctuary for a numerous variety of plant and animal species. Exploring those fiords by manner of boat or kayak permits web web page site visitors to immerse themselves within the serenity and majesty of the natural environment.

The Southern Alps and Fiordland regions are not handiest visually stunning however also offer a selection of out of doors amusement sports activities. Hiking and tramping trails, in conjunction with the Milford Track and the Routeburn Track, provide opportunities to experience the wilderness up near and appreciate the area's natural beauty. These trails show off the shape of landscapes, from alpine meadows to ancient beech forests and glacial valleys.

The Southern Alps and Fiordland are also havens for adventure lovers. Mountaineering, skiing, heli-snowboarding, and paragliding are famous sports activities, attracting thrill-seekers who need to mission themselves in the direction of the dramatic and annoying terrain.

The importance of the Southern Alps and Fiordland extends beyond their physical splendor. These areas are of cultural and non secular importance to the indigenous Māori human beings. They are woven into Māori folklore and legends, symbolizing the electricity and presence of ancestral spirits and gods.

Efforts to protect and hold the Southern Alps and Fiordland had been made via the reputation quo of national parks and conservation regions. Aoraki/Mount Cook National Park, Fiordland National Park, and Westland Tai Poutini National Park guard those herbal wonders and ensure their persisted lifestyles for future generations to comprehend and experience.

The Southern Alps and Fiordland are testament to the long-lasting power of nature and its potential to encourage awe and wonder. These majestic landscapes characteristic reminders of the considerable forces which have fashioned New Zealand's geology and preserve to captivate all who've the privilege to experience their grandeur.

Fiery Mountains and Volcanic Wonders: Geology of New Zealand

New Zealand's geology is a testament to the dynamic forces that have long-set up the united states of the us's panorama over loads of loads of years. The land is famend for its fiery mountains, volcanic wonders, and precise geological abilities, showcasing the effective and ever-evolving nature of the Earth's geology.

The geology of New Zealand is a give up end result of its region at the boundary of two tectonic plates: the Pacific Plate and the Australian Plate. The collision and interplay of these plates have given rise to a numerous sort of geological phenomena, together with volcanic hobby, earthquakes, and the formation of mountain degrees.

Volcanoes are amazing skills of New Zealand's geology. The u . S . Is domestic to a tremendous type of energetic and dormant volcanoes, that have finished a important characteristic in shaping the land and developing its specific landscape. The North Island, mainly, is famend for its volcanic hobby, with the Taupo Volcanic Zone being one of the most energetic volcanic areas within the global.

Mount Ruapehu, located in the important North Island, is one in each of New Zealand's most iconic and active volcanoes. Its towering presence and commonplace volcanic hobby entice web site visitors and scientists alike. The close by Tongariro National Park, a UNESCO World Heritage internet site on line, showcases a cluster of volcanoes, alongside aspect Mount Ngauruhoe, that is famous for its appearance within the "Lord of the Rings" film trilogy.

White Island, positioned off the coast of the Bay of Plenty, is each different well-known active volcano in New Zealand. Its volcanic hobby creates a totally specific and frequently surreal panorama, characterised via steaming vents, acidic crater lakes, and an otherworldly environment.

The geothermal hobby in New Zealand is some different wonderful trouble of its geology. Rotorua, within the North Island, is famous for its geothermal wonders, together with effervescent mud swimming pools, warm springs, and geysers. The area's geothermal power is harnessed for various capabilities, together with heating and power technology.

The Southern Alps, extending through the South Island, are a prominent mountain variety shaped by using way of tectonic forces and uplift. These majestic mountains are a prevent end result of the collision among the Pacific and Australian Plates. Mount Cook, the very first-rate top in New Zealand, stands proudly within this variety, achieving a towering top of three,724 meters.

Glaciers have additionally completed a good sized characteristic in shaping the geology of New Zealand. The Southern Alps are adorned with exceptional glaciers, together with the Franz Josef Glacier and the Fox Glacier. These big rivers of ice have carved deep valleys and left in the back of breathtaking landscapes, developing a placing assessment in opposition to the luxurious rainforests underneath.

The South Island's West Coast is famend for its rugged and wild shoreline, unique with the useful resource of the relentless pounding of the Tasman Sea. The erosion because of the waves has created dramatic cliffs, sea stacks, and herbal arches, including to the visible splendor of the area.

The geological interest in New Zealand isn't always constrained to the mainland. The u.S.'s offshore islands, such as the subantarctic Auckland Islands and the volcanic White Island, offer similarly insights into the numerous and dynamic geology of the area.

Earthquakes are a normal function of New Zealand's geology due to its role on a tectonic plate boundary. The u . S . A .

Reports masses of earthquakes every one year, regardless of the fact that most are minor and bypass neglected. However, brilliant earthquakes have shaped the state's records and impacted its infrastructure. The devastating earthquakes in Napier in 1931 and Christchurch in 2010 and 2011 serve as reminders of the u . S . A .'s seismic vulnerability.

New Zealand's geology is a topic of medical research and observe, attracting geologists and researchers from throughout the arena. The precise geological capabilities, volcanic hobby, and tectonic plate interactions offer a wealth of information approximately the Earth's strategies and the evolution of landscapes.

The geology of New Zealand isn't fine a systematic fascination however furthermore an essential a part of the u . S .'s cultural and environmental ancient past. Māori mythology and legends frequently encompass geological capabilities, attributing religious importance to mountains, lakes, and rivers. The land's geological range additionally contributes to New Zealand's wealthy biodiversity, helping unique ecosystems and habitats.

In end, New Zealand's geology is a fascinating tapestry of fiery mountains, volcanic wonders, and geological talents usual via the use of using tectonic forces, glaciers, and erosion. The united states of america of the us's numerous landscapes and dynamic geological tactics maintain to inspire awe and provide a glimpse into the profound forces that shape our planet.

Chapter 8: The Treaty Of Waitangi Revisited

The Treaty of Waitangi, signed on February 6, 1840, among representatives of the British Crown and severa Māori chiefs, remains a huge record in New Zealand's records. The treaty have come to be intended to establish a foundation for peaceful coexistence, outline the connection between Māori and the Crown, and make certain the safety of Māori rights, land, and sovereignty.

The Treaty of Waitangi includes variations: the English model and the Māori version. While the Māori model is considered the authoritative textual content, there are variations in interpretation and translation many of the versions, important to ongoing debates and discussions about the treaty's which means that that and purpose.

One of the key elements addressed inside the Treaty of Waitangi is the problem of land. The treaty diagnosed and confident the continuing ownership and possession of land thru Māori. It acknowledged the importance of land to Māori identity, way of life, and health. However, differing interpretations and subsequent land transactions triggered top notch land loss for Māori over time.

The treaty moreover hooked up the idea of sovereignty, acknowledging the authority of the British Crown over New Zealand on the same time as spotting the persevering with authority and autonomy of Māori chiefs and their tribes. The specific knowledge of sovereignty and its implications had been hassle to differing interpretations and ongoing discussions, shaping the relationship amongst Māori and the Crown.

In the years following the signing of the treaty, tensions arose as European settlers arrived in increasing numbers and sought to accumulate land for settlement and improvement. Land purchases and conflicts over land possession induced large annoying situations and grievances for Māori businesses, as their lands have been frequently curious about out proper session or trustworthy reimbursement.

The land troubles addressed within the Treaty of Waitangi keep to have profound implications for New Zealand society. Land claims, called Treaty of Waitangi claims or Treaty settlements, were pursued via the usage of Māori tribes searching for redress for ancient land loss, breaches of the treaty, and different grievances. These settlements purpose to cope with past injustices and promote reconciliation and partnership among Māori and the Crown.

The Waitangi Tribunal, installed in 1975, plays a critical function inside the choice of treaty-associated grievances. It is an unbiased body tasked with investigating and making recommendations on Treaty of Waitangi claims. The tribunal's findings and pointers inform the treaty settlement technique, contributing to the recovery of land and the recognition of Māori rights and pursuits.

The treaty has been revisited and its ideas affirmed thru numerous jail and political dispositions. The Treaty of Waitangi Act 1975, for instance, diagnosed the treaty as a dwelling document and provided a framework for its interpretation and alertness in modern New Zealand. The treaty concepts, which include the thoughts of partnership, participation, and protection, were said in law, insurance, and choice-making methods.

The interpretation and alertness of the Treaty of Waitangi continue to be complicated and evolving issues. The ideas of the treaty are important to fashionable discussions on constitutional arrangements, governance, aid management, and the protection of indigenous rights. Efforts to beautify the data, understand, and implementation of the treaty's thoughts stay ongoing.

The Treaty of Waitangi and its implications for land and sovereignty are topics of ongoing reflected photograph, speak, and debate in New Zealand. The journey in the direction of actual partnership, reconciliation, and the popularity of Māori rights and interests is a shared duty for all New Zealanders, and the treaty offers a framework for shaping a more inclusive and equitable society.

In conclusion, the Treaty of Waitangi represents an crucial ancient agreement among Māori and the British Crown, addressing land and sovereignty. Its interpretation and application preserve to form the connection amongst Māori and the Crown, and efforts to cope with ancient grievances and promote reconciliation are ongoing. The treaty stays a residing file, guiding New Zealand in the direction of a destiny primarily based mostly on mutual recognize, partnership, and the popularity of Māori rights and aspirations.

Women's Suffrage: Trailblazers of Equality

The journey towards ladies's suffrage in New Zealand is a testomony to the willpower, courage, and resilience of trailblazing girls who fought for equal rights and political illustration. The success of girls's suffrage in New Zealand modified into a awesome milestone in the international battle for gender equality and stays a source of idea and pleasure.

The movement for ladies's suffrage obtained momentum within the past due nineteenth century as women commenced out advocating for his or her right to participate within the democratic method. Prior to 1893, girls in New Zealand, like in masses of different nations, had been denied the right to vote and take part in political reviews absolutely primarily based on their gender.

Kate Sheppard, a distinguished suffragette and social reformer, emerged as a crucial determine inside the marketing campaign for girls's suffrage. Sheppard's control, persuasive advocacy, and strategic organizing have been instrumental in rallying resource and elevating interest approximately the importance of women's political rights.

The suffrage movement in New Zealand won big help from each girls and sympathetic guys. Petitions, conferences, and public demonstrations have come to be effective device to mobilize public opinion and call for political alternate. In 1893, a chain of a achievement petitions containing approximately 32,000 signatures have been furnished to Parliament, urging the government to offer women the right to vote.

The tireless efforts of suffragettes and their allies culminated inside the passing of the Electoral Act in September 1893, making New Zealand the number one self-governing united states in the worldwide to offer ladies the right to vote in national elections. This groundbreaking achievement positioned New Zealand at the forefront of the worldwide women's suffrage movement and set an inspiring example for distinctive global locations to follow.

The effect of ladies's suffrage prolonged beyond the political sphere. The reputation of ladies's proper to vote modified right into a huge step toward gender equality and social exchange. It opened doors for women to actively participate in public existence, voice their problems, and make a contribution to shaping the dominion's future.

Following the fulfillment of suffrage, ladies in New Zealand continued to interrupt barriers and challenge gender norms. In 1893, Elizabeth McCombs have emerge as the number one woman elected to the New Zealand Parliament, paving the manner for future generations of girls to pursue political careers. Since then, girls have held splendid positions in politics, in conjunction with serving as Prime Minister, Governor-General, and Members of Parliament at some stage in numerous events.

The effect of ladies's suffrage in New Zealand reverberated beyond national borders. The fulfillment of the suffrage movement stimulated women around the arena and strengthened the worldwide fight for girls's rights and suffrage. New Zealand's achievement have become a symbol of desire and development, influencing next suffrage actions in international locations which consist of Australia, the UK, and the US.

The legacy of girls's suffrage in New Zealand is one in every of progress, empowerment, and ongoing advocacy for gender equality. The proper to vote furnished a platform for ladies to deal with broader problems of social justice, along with access to education, employment opportunities, and reproductive rights.

In recognition of the importance of women's suffrage, the Suffrage Centennial have grow to be celebrated in 1993, marking a hundred years considering the reality that New Zealand have emerge as the primary united states of america to provide women the right to vote. The centennial birthday party served as a reminder of the sacrifices, electricity of will, and achievements of the suffragettes, and as a name to hold striving for gender equality and women's empowerment.

Women's suffrage stays a foundational success in New Zealand's data, representing a pivotal second inside the ongoing pursuit of gender equality. The contributions and struggles of the suffragettes preserve to encourage generations of ladies and men to recommend for same rights, assignment societal norms, and paintings in the course of a extra inclusive and equitable society for all.

In end, the women's suffrage motion in New Zealand was a extremely good financial disaster in the the us's records, marked by using way of the brave efforts of suffragettes who fought for equal rights and political example. The success of ladies's suffrage in 1893 changed into a notable milestone that resonated globally and contributed to the ongoing combat for gender equality. The legacy of girls's suffrage continues to encourage and remind us of the importance of empowering ladies and spotting their essential contributions to society.

Chapter 9: The Maori Settlement

Before the Europeans first came into New Zealand, the Maori were the primary humans to ever inhabit the region inside the 10th century AD. At that factor, the united states of a come to be named Aotearoa – because of this the "Land of the Long, White Cloud." According to Maori folklore, the primary character to ever acquire New Zealand become someone named Kupe, who ventured in the course of the Pacific in his voyaging canoe (waka hourua) and used the sea currents and the stars as his guide for navigation. Leaving his ancestral land of Hawaiki in are seeking out of new lands, he's concept to have made his landfall nearly a thousand years in the past at the Northland Hokianga Harbor.

The Formation of the Maori Tribes

After Kupe's arrival, extra human beings from Hawaiki arrived. Their area of shipping is not determined on any maps these days – but it is believed that the island (or islands) became discovered within the South Pacific Ocean – mainly, in Polynesia. This perception is because of the similarities among the Maori language, as well as one-of-a-kind customs of Polynesia. Islands of basis are idea to be Hawaii, Cook Island, and Tahiti.

It is idea that the migration has now not been unplanned, but in fact, planned. The canoes saved migrating from side to side from the islands – making Hawaiki their very last agreement. The first seven tribes that arrived in the land of Aotearoa have been referred to as Te Arawa, Tainui, Tokomau, Kurahapuo, Mataatua, Takitimu, and Aotea. The society modified into tribal, and all and sundry belonged to a family (of their language, whanau), which end up in truth a sub-tribe of the principle tribe. The subtribe became known as hapu, whilst the primary tribe turned into iwi.

The Maori and Warfare

The Maori have been furthermore warriors of a kind. They fought using a kind of long membership made from wooden named taiah, but additionally short golf equipment referred to as patu. The human beings additionally fought brief clubs made from jade which they referred to as mere. These weapons have been pretty durable and much much less prone to being damaged as compared to a wooden membership – but the pinnacle material have end up as a substitute tough to locate. Only people who had been relatively excessive-up in the tribe have been commonly able to get their arms on this sort of weapon.

Warfare turned into pretty commonplace within the Maori tribes, especially in the pre-European times. The warriors were fearless and strong and evolved exceptional talents in dealing with their traditional guns – which precipitated the confrontations to be countless. The descendants can also no longer be the use of the ones weapons in fight, however they have got remained ingrained in the vintage traditions. For instance, those tools may be seen in Maori ceremonies, one in each of them being the wero (because of this task).

Aside from taking the offensive, the Maori had been additionally quite genuine at making plans the defensive. For instance, to protect themselves from attacks led thru using special essential tribes (iwi), they will build a pa or a fortified village. The pa would be constructed in strategic locations, having a chain of trenches and stockades that would keep the intruders from coming in. The population is probably saved regular this manner. Nowadays, the descendants are no longer constructing pa structures, but you can although find numerous pa internet web sites all throughout New Zealand.

Most of the time, the Maori have been beneath war with the Moriori – which have come to be additionally a Polynesian tribe, and a peace-loving one, for that rely. This tribe inhabited the Chatham Islands, which have become a few 900 km distance from the Christchurch. It is idea that this tribe migrated from the South part of New Zealand – and thru the 18th century, there were about 2000 Moriori on the lands. However, attacks from the Maori, in addition to ailment caused this tribe to die out, its final complete-blooded member taking their last breath in 1993.

Survival and Agriculture

Aside from being very expert at warfare, the Maori had one more aspect that they've been quite correct at – and that turned into "survival." Since they have been professional fishermen and hunters, there was normally no hassle with bringing food to the table. They moreover knew a way to make the tremendous system for this task – which encompass a internet crafted from harakeke (which have become flax), or stone/bone-carved fishhooks.

With these equipment, they had been capable of seize some of the sizable materials of the sea. Most of the time, they looked for dolphins, seals, and whales – but additionally they went for everyday fish in addition to shellfish. They additionally hunted a form of large, flightless chook known as moa which lived just down the coast, however the ones birds ultimately have grow to be extinct.

They delivered a desire of factors with them as they migrated to New Zealand. For one, they added dogs, however further they introduced rats with them in 1350 AD – specially, the kiore. Whereas most humans noticed rats as pests they desired to remove, the Maori noticed subjects instead in a extraordinary way. They found the kiore as a completely essential supply of food, and that they have been joyous of the reality that this small rat managed to evolve to this new land.

The Maori moreover delivered gourds and candy potatoes with them – and replenished their food plan with the aid of way of eating fern roots. They had a sincere variety of neighborhood vegetables, berries, and roots to move for – due to this that meals have become in no manner sincerely an problem within the new land. You fine needed to understand a way to maintain yourself and in which to find out right food.

Once stuck and/or collected, the ones components were carried the use of woven baskets – and will normally be saved interior a pataka. This changed right right into a sort of storehouse that is probably raised on stilts to maintain it secure from vermin and other scavenging wild animals. Most of the time, the ones patakas held elaborate wooden carving – some element they were also especially right at.

They also used to make tikis and pendants from whalebone. The Maori have been additionally pretty famous for their tattoos and moko, which used a mallet, bone chisel, and blue pigments.

Chapter 10: The First Europeans In New Zealand

The first European to ever set foot in New Zealand has come to be a Dutch explorer called Abel Tasman. This is probably why the u . S . Has acquired this form of Dutch-sounding call, due to the fact the primary human beings used to name it "Nieuw Zeeland." This discovery becomes made on December thirteenth, 1642 – and even as the European settlers have been curious approximately this new land, the Maori were not within the slightest glad approximately those invaders. Continuous fights between the European and the war-educated Maori made the Europeans no longer so eager to transport lower back to this land.

For this purpose, the Europeans left New Zealand on my own – at least until round 1762, even as British explorer James Cook arrived alongside with his supply called

The Endeavor. As anticipated, the primary encounters with the Maori were now not in the least peaceful — but very violent, because the Maori were looking to protect their land. Cook ended up calling that area "Poverty Bay," and he saved crusing closer to a unique tour spot.

Arriving at Mercury Bay, but, topics began out changing. Cook have turn out to be friends with the community Maori, whose interest obtained over the violence and worry of invasion. After interacting with that precise iwi, Cook started out out exploring New Zealand and mapped it correctly.

Cook made voyages to New Zealand in advance than the rest of the Europeans came in — the number one being in 1773 and the second one in 1777. After that, first-rate human beings have end up inquisitive about this "New Zeeland," and one of a kind explorers were quick to follow – the primary being the French, discovered closely by using the Spanish.

The Relationship among Tribes and European Settlers

As the 18th century changed into turning a ultra-modern leaf, increasingly sailors have been starting to arrive in New Zealand, looking for a present day day life. The Maori have been simply no longer surely content material material fabric with the Europeans arriving on their land – however they had been slightly masses tons much less violent compared to the beginnings.

Beginning with the nineteenth century, new businesses started out out to arrive. This time, it changed into a collection of whalers, which saw potential inside the new land. Sailors commenced decreasing timber from New Zealand for his or her spas and masts, and a smaller agency of settlers made their domestic right here. Around this time, some of those Europeans is probably searching for land from the Maori humans.

Generally, the connection a number of the Maori and the Europeans became quite non violent – but there have been despite the fact that remoted conflicts that precipitated tension among the 2 groups. Not all natives had been satisfied about those "invaders" trying to find to take over their lands, so they were looking for to exert domination.

In most instances, the Maori and the Europeans did try to help every extremely good. The Maori gave the Europeans flax and meals in exchange for European items – muskets included. However, the imported muskets made the struggle with the Maori even greater heated – principal all the manner into the Musket wars that lasted from 1819 until 1825.

There have been right and bads of their relationship. The Europeans did convey illnesses to which the Maori had no resistance – inflicting a number of them to die out. Still, similarly they brought pigs and potatoes – which they shared with the Maori tribes.

New Laws in New Zealand

In 1817, subjects have been starting to alternate due to the fact the New South Wales legal suggestions began out extending to New Zealand. Even with this, subjects weren't clearly in order – and the prison hints have been no longer helping them inside the slightest. This is why some of the European settlers asked for aid from the British authorities. As a quit stop end result of this request, the authorities despatched James Busby to behave as an "legitimate British Resident" in New Zealand.

Seeing as the Government had concerns concerning the manner wherein the Europeans sold land from the Maori, they favored to alter the approach nicely. In truth, Busby's undertaking have become to unite the tribes of the Maori and turn them proper right into a unmarried federation – one that the British authorities may also want to without trouble deal with. Busby changed into changed through William Hobson in 1838.

In the start, the British government had their reservations approximately making New Zealand a colony – however once they noticed that the French have been approximately to do the same element, they modified their thoughts brief. This would possibly deliver rights to every occasions – however severa regulations would moreover be worried.

The Decline of the Maori

As years have exceeded, an increasing number of colonists were arriving in New Zealand – growing some of provinces wherein the Europeans may settle. These settlers delivered with them sheep – and as the flocks of sheep started growing, the organization additionally have turn out to be notable for the Europeans. Add to this the gold rush of the 1860s, and the colonists in New Zealand were beginning to have a fairly specific life.

At that factor, New Zealand's white population grew as an opportunity big. By the time 1861 became a nook, the population emerge as round 100,000. About 20 years later, that populace pretty grew to 500,000 – causing the Maori to be alternatively discontented. New Maori kings had been appointed, and battle broke out after that.

The Maori numbers were delivered down via conflict – and their inexistent resistance to the European illnesses did no longer assist their reason. When James Cook first arrived, there have been about 100,000 Maori in New Zealand. However, in 1896, their numbers dropped a lot that there have been satisfactory approximately 40, 000 of them left.

Chapter 11: The Treaty Of Waitangi And The Colony Changes

Within only some days after arriving in New Zealand, William Hobson commenced to draft some of the most vital documents in the u . S . A .'s records – taken into consideration one among them being the Treaty of Waitangi. Considering the large scale of transactions that had been taking region at the lands of New Zealand, the government decided that in an effort to protect every the Maori and the British settlers, some order and rules must want to be brought upon.

The Implications of the Treaty of Waitangi

Practically talking, the Treaty of Waitangi come to be – and is – a widespread announcement that contained principles on which every the Maori and the British determined to create a political compact. In specific phrases, the 2 had been expected to grow to be a country simply so they may all construct a logo-new government in New Zealand.

This treaty functions 3 articles. In the English report, it is cited that the Maori will cede New Zealand sovereignty to Britain. In particular terms, the Crown is probably given proper to buy and promote the belongings from the Maori – and in go again, the Maori will get hold of rightful possession in their lands and ownership. The Maori can also have the equal rights as a British problem.

In unique terms, the Treaty of Waitangi might defend the rights of both the Maori and the British with the useful resource of:

Accepting the reality that the Maori tribes have the proper to organizing themselves, in addition to of protecting their manner of lifestyles and beneficial useful resource manage.

Pushing the Government to behave in high-quality religion and fairly in the direction of the participants of the Maori tribes.

Requiring that the government is responsible for supporting the ones which can be addressing the grievance.

Establishing that each Maori and non-Maori are equal beneath the New Zealand legal suggestions.

This report modified into supplied to the Maori gatherings at the grounds of Busby's home – one that modified into determined at Waitangi. The execs and cons of this report were debated for an entire day and an entire night time time, with all forty Maori tribe chiefs searching for to determine whether or not or no longer the treaty became a good deal for them or not. Eventually, they decided for the treaty, and on February 6, 1840, the final file become signed.

By the time September became a nook, round 500 distinct Maori have also signed severa copies of the treaty, sending it in the course of New Zealand. Eventually, starting with 1840, New Zealand stopped functioning beneath the control of New South Wales and have end up its non-public colony – with Hobson acting as its governor.

Language Differences in the Treaty

At that point, the Treaty of Waitangi modified into seemed as a founding report of New Zeeland – however it also introduced approximately splendid controversy ever due to the fact the instant it emerge as signed. The language versions a number of the Maori and the English versions of the treaty are what truely sparked those debates. The British claimed that through signing the treaty, the Maori ceded their sovereignty – but non-stop warfare proved that the dreams of the colonists had been nice secondary to the needs of the Maori. Granted, at that point, there have been greater Maori than there were colonists – so the Maori believed this to be the natural order of factors.

Furthermore, the this means that of the word "sovereignty" differs from lifestyle to way of life. For instance, in the Maori way of life, sovereignty is translated as kawanatanga – due to this "governance." Some of the Maori that signed the record believed that they'll give up their land's government – but may want to nevertheless have the proper to manipulate their affairs. The English model promised "undisturbed possession" of the "homes" that that they'd, while the Maori article promised tino rangatiratanga (meaning "entire authority") over all of the taonga (which is probably "treasures," whether they may be intangible or no longer).

The statistics of the Maori was pretty lots at odds with the knowledge of the British negotiation – and due to the fact the Maori took price within the spoken word, a few in addition causes need to were so as. Most of the time, most Maori understood the phrases and claimed that they have all been honored. Others, but, have now not asked the right questions beforehand – and characteristic protested with the aid of manner of marching in the direction of the Parliament and occupying the land there.

Suffice to mention, this file end up aimed to be a "safety act" for the Maori, but for the settlers as properly. This treaty was a manner of bringing some order right into a land with none actual recommendations –

for putting in place a way of lifestyles so that no revolts could be breaking out. While sometimes there is probably "hiccups" to the device, most of the time, the phrases might be venerated — specifically due to the truth the Maori and the colonists agreed that the quality manner to stay to tell the story modified into to learn how to stay with each other.

Chapter 12: The New Zealand Wars

Peace would not final indefinitely – and the primary attack at the Crown may want to observe quickly after the treaty grow to be signed. In 1845, Hone Heke fired the number one assaults at Kororareka, sparking the Northern War – and the first actual struggle of New Zealand. Heke had the opinion that the Maori no longer had any privileges and status over their land – and that the British took declare of the whole lot, no matter what end up stated inside the Treaty of Waitangi.

This Northern War might mark the begin of what would further on be called the New Zealand wars. It changed into a struggle that noticed round 3000 lethal casualties – maximum of them being Maori. The majority died in an try to guard their lands. However, maximum of them may want to extremely good friend with different colonists – accomplishing character sub-tribe dreams even on the price of the precept tribes. The battle lasted for a chunk over a long time, with instances of peace that might nearly constitute the tranquility earlier than a storm.

The Kind Movement

Following the Treaty of Waitangi, a instead uneasy duration of peace observed. The uneasiness have grow to be due to the settler populace that endured to covet for the lands excited about the aid of the Maori. After 365 days, the pressure started to heighten – in most cases after the Parliament of New Zealand commenced to advantage responsible government. Most of the Parliament people believed that their allegiance lied with the settlers – the folks that honestly elected them. The Colonial Office moreover believed that New Zealand might should pay its percentage – and this will be completed by way of the usage of having more agreement land from the Maori tribes.

On the land of the South Island – a place in which Maori could probably live – settlers at the facet in their sheep started out spreading effectively. Still, this did no longer exercise to the North Island, seeing that during 1860 the Maori regardless of the reality that had 80% of the lands. Because of this, the colonists can be cooped in settlements across the coast. The fact that some Maori went into business enterprise farming moreover did now not do lots to ease the disappointment of the settlers. To them, the lands that have been owned by way of the Mori were lands that were unoccupied (i.E. "wastelands").

To counter the non-stop pressure that they acquired to promote the land, the Maori recommended that their land have to be located under the safety of a unmarried discern — a king. Te Wherowhero of the Waikato — someone that had no longer previously signed the treaty of Waitangi, have become the primary King of the Maori in 1858.

The "King Movement" (furthermore called the Kingitanga) have become an try to unite the tribes underneath a single banner — but maximum most vital tribes (iwi) refused to discard their mana honestly so they could be part of a few other one. Unlike maximum settlers and the colonial government, the Kingitanga have become not supposed to be an competition movement in opposition to the queen — however as an opportunity, one intended to shield their lands from being claimed.

The War of Taranaki and Waikato

The period of uneasiness persevered most of the Maori and the settlers – until ultimately, battle broke out in Taranaki in 1860. This changed into because of the selection interested about the useful resource of Thomas Gore Brown, the Governor of New Zealand, to buy land furnished through a minor chief (Te Ati Awa). This provide was disputed with the aid of better chiefs – and ultimately, New Plymouth have become besieged. Once this came about, the British tried to supply the Maori proper into a decisive conflict. After the warriors from Waikato additionally have come to be worried, worry of a miles wider struggle has further on been raised. Both parties agreed to a truce in 1861, and George Grey was reinstated for a 2nd term due to the truth the Governor. Peace, but, isn't always prolonged-lasting, as hostilities in Taranaki might yet again flare up in 1863 – right on the eve of George Grey's Waikato invasion.

July 1863 is the month whilst the War of Waikato broke out. In the seven months that followed, the British forces attempted to push their way inside the course of the south, into the agricultural base of the Kingitanga. They captured numerous ambitious pa along the manner however additionally took preserve of a pa that became unmanned. They advanced in the land – and in 1864, they defeated the Kingitanga opponents that have been led into warfare with the aid of way of Rewi Maniapoto.

The hobby became now grew to come to be onto the Bay of Plenty and Tauranga – who seemed like an clean target, as the iwi had definitely despatched reinforcements to the Kingitanga. The British forces held an overwhelming benefit in both firepower and numbers, however they suffered an embarrassing and demoralizing defeat on the Gate Pa (Pukehinahina). However, they later had been given their revenge on the Te Ranga, wherein the advertising and marketing marketing campaign truely got here to an stop.

The settlers on the South Island refused to help pay for the battles taking region in the North and best desired the subjects to be resolved. As the Gold Rush become retreating in the South, some of the settlers started questioning whether or not or not or not they need to cut up New Zealand into colonies or not – the North and the South.

A New Conflict

The conflict of Waikato came to an give up – but this did now not endorse that New Zealand observed the final of war. In fact, this battle commenced out brewing as quick as Pai Marire emerged in 1862. This exceedingly new non secular religion had commenced making itself regarded beginning with the Taranaki battle, and the warfare associated with it. However, for max of the Europeans, this motion became quite plenty synonymous with hostility and violence in the path of the settlers.

In 1868, greater stopping broke out – this time associated with the prophet warriors Titokowaru and Te Kooti. These "guerilla campaigns," as they were called, went through maximum of the North Island, going from the center to the east and west coasts. This time, the military resources of the colony were stretched nearly to a breaking problem.

However, at the identical time as Titokowaru had infinite ideal victories with the resource of February 1869, his entire army became disintegrated almost in a unmarried day. Maori King Tawhiao granted him sanctuary in 1872 – but that modified into also a glide that delivered the war to an surrender. After that, in 1881, Tawhiao himself managed to make peace with the crown – leaving Rohe Potae (the King Country) and returning to Waikato.

The Confiscations of Lands

After the battle had come to an end, a new struggle got here in the shape of the raupatu – or the land confiscations phase. The consequences were specific from one place to some other. People from the Waikato-Tainui tribes felt the ones consequences the maximum – but so did special tribes as nicely. The navy settlers may also hold to confiscate lands – appearing consequently as a buffer a few of the European Maori businesses.

Even the Maori that became declared as "reliable" had their lands confiscated. Plus, those who but retained ownership in their land had been imposed new British notions that would have an effect on their ownership. Needless to mention, this added on a wave of small riots, as none of those affected were glad about this final results.

Starting with 1879, Parihaka's Taranaki agreement became identified due to the fact the middle that become against confiscation. The leaders of this employer, Tohu Kakaki, and Te Whiti o Rongomai recommended their fanatics to begin uprooting the survey pegs, however furthermore to erect fences and plow up roads on the lands that they taken into consideration to be theirs.

Most of the time, the resistance have emerge as non violent – however arrests had been even though made previous to the Government's invasion of Parihaka nearing the give up of 1881. Armed forces raided the defenseless settlements, and each Te Whiti o Rogomai and Tohu Kakahi were captured and despatched into exile in the South Island.

During the two many years that this conflict spread over, quite some Maori land ended up being confiscated. It additionally introduced on the form of Maori to drop significantly – which started out out to be a problem, seeing as there have been already fewer Maori than there had been Europeans.

Chapter 13: The Economic Expansion Of New Zealand

The warfare had hit the pause button on any development that the North Island need to have made. While this doesn't advocate that the North can also want to not get better, it although gave the South a head start. Thanks to this, the South Island have become the number one issue of New Zealand's economic machine.

Prosperity within the South Island

In Canterbury, wool manufacturing had reached a immoderate top – making the vicinity the wealthiest province that New Zealand had. Furthermore, in Dunedin, adjustments have been also going on – mainly due to the gold rush. Gold became placed in 1860-1861 in Central Otago, remodeling Dunedin into one in every of the most essential cities in New Zealand.

During this time, many younger guys — hundreds of them, sincerely — rushed to Otago in the hopes that they will find out gold and create a fortune. Gold changed into additionally found within the North Island, inflicting the gold rush to grow even more potent. A extraordinarily small wide variety of humans "struck fortune," so to speak, but the collective charge of gold that turn out to be located had controlled to stimulate the financial system of New Zealand.

These traits did plenty to attract the younger, male population of New Zealand — all of which had left in a "rush" to strike it rich. However, the government believed that the only manner to benefit long-time period fortune might be to consciousness on the stability and order supplied with the resource of lifestyles in a own family. Therefore, many schemes had been used to attract the lady migrants as nicely —

especially the ladies whose guys had come trying to find gold. Allowing them to create a circle of relatives can also assist society flourish.

In the 1870s, many people observed that they will discover new life in New Zealand. Thanks to the assist from the authorities, masses of British human beings controlled to earn a proper dwelling. The production of railways made transportation and commuting much less difficult, and towns stored appearing or extended.

In 1881, New Zealand officially makes the number one shipment to England – one containing frozen meat. As exporting meat on the facet of cheese and butter have become a possibility, New Zealand have come to be sincerely one of Britain's important companies. Since most of New Zealand's financial device emerge as based totally on farming and agriculture, they proved to be a reasonably dependable deliver.

The Vogel Plan

Just like many other frontier societies, New Zealand emerge as moreover at risk of the whims of a useful useful resource-based financial system. Gold manufacturing commenced out to fall in 1860, and the wool charges furthermore began to slide. Things were searching pretty lousy for the financial system.

This is wherein the Colonial Treasurer Julius Vogel stepped in. In 1870, he proposed a alternatively bold improvement plan in which New Zealand ought to borrow huge sums of coins from England. That cash might be used to assist the migrants settle and purchase extra lands from the Maori. They should invest that money into public paintings, developing an infrastructure that is crucial for an super economic system. They may want to construct roads, railways, port facilities, bridges, and telegraph strains – some thing that would help installation and raise the monetary device.

The critical piece of Vogel's plan have become the promise to assemble around 1600 km (a thousand miles) of railways – all over the direction of 9 years. Until 1870, New Zealand had spherical 7 km of railway strains – however via 1880, the ones railways had expanded to 2000 km. This supplied get entry to to numerous far off regions, at the side of the Paheha agreement. More British migrants got here flooding, and the populace of the colony almost doubled in its duration over the following ten years.

The Vogel era additionally marked the finale of the provincial government – which became at the top of the political opinions ever given that 1850. The new era that has been made available changed into starting to push away the "tyranny of distance," as they referred to as it – which nice partly justified the formation of all the one of a kind provinces.

The reality that the provincial government grow to be abolished in 1876 controlled to provide New Zealand some reputation. It is probably visible as development, proving that a single usa would likely don't have any want for provincial parochialism.

Seeing that this became no matter the truth that the put up-war duration, this decade become an era of instructional improvement. Several Native Schools were raised as much as replace the undertaking schooling every Maori used to undertake. The universities of New Zealand and Otago moreover came to be for folks that favored a better schooling. However, at this issue, the training but had to be paid for – so at the identical time as the

Education Act of 1877 came earlier, many gates had been opened. The public college device turn out to be taking form, and those have to get less complex get proper of get right of entry to to to education.

The Economic Depression

It grow to be right that Vogel have emerge as certainly a kingdom-giant visionary – however he changed into but a parent crowded in controversy at that time. In 1878, the colony slipped into a very prolonged economic depression – and maximum humans blamed it on Vogel's plan to borrow from Britain. The expenses for farm merchandise furthermore fell, and the market for the land become no longer as sturdy because it became as soon as.

There have come to be a better price of unemployment in the city areas than it ever changed into earlier than. Women and children alike have been exploited and made to go through quite some difficult hard paintings in bad taking walks environments. There were even questions about how New Zealand ought to offer help for the terrible. The welfare america changed into nearly nonexistent, and the charitable beneficial aid come to be simply now not sufficient to assist they all.

During those tough times, the households were starting to look for new techniques to enhance their manner of life. They began to talk approximately whether or not alcohol had any area in New Zealand existence or now not. It have become believed that alcohol – liquor, to be greater particular – made the men forget about about what their obligations have been. A temperance and prohibition motion sprang up and continued to unfold as they tried to restrict the suffering of the ladies. Many women and kids had fallen victim to alcohol abuse, specially because the fathers would possibly indulge too much in liquor. At that factor, the fight for enfranchising ladies seemed to be more and more vital. The advertising and marketing marketing campaign modified right into a success, and in 1893, New Zealand grow to be the number one u.S. Of the usa in the global to provide ladies vote casting right inside the national elections.

Chapter 14: The Liberal Age

Now that women had vote casting rights, plural vote casting became taken off the desk and each ladies and men may want to vote inside the electorates that they owned property in. At the same time, a completely great episode within the information of New Zealand started brewing – being located at the backdrop of New Zealand's first usa-full-size strike. During that point, employees from all the ports might prevent their work, step out, and offer assist for the unionists of Australia. However, that have become the initial plan.

This maritime strike added on a sincere quantity of disruption within the trading performed through way of the colony, as well as to the transportation networks. The elegance recognition surely grew inside a few personnel – but in the long run, the 3-month strike resulted in prefer of the seamen and those who have been allied with them.

After the elections of 1890, the Parliament met on the begin of 1891. Known because the first political party in New Zealand, the Liberals (who got here out a fulfillment) stood in the lower back of John Ballance. After Ballance died, the manipulate went to Richard John Seddon. "King Dick", as he emerge as popularly referred to as, modified into in rate of New Zealand's political panorama for about 13 years – and the Liberals stood in electricity until approximately 1912. The social and economic reforms that they went through, together with the egalitarian rhetoric, allowed the Liberals to form their political time table and take it properly into the twentieth century.

The Liberals persisted to accumulate help from the revenue-earners within the city vicinity – however additionally from those residing on small farms and in provincial towns. An financial healing based totally mostly on export also started out to take shape. The liberals saw farming as a way to gain from export – and not as a way of supplementing the contemporary profits of those living in small houses.

The reason of the liberal policy modified into to assist small farmers gain a settlement. In their eyes, this could be achieved most effective with the aid of subdividing the "big estates" that have been currently on the South Island. In the imaginative and prescient that the Liberals had for "God's private u . S . A .," they noticed that more Maori land can be used for settlement. John McKenzie, the minister of lands, agreed that masses of Maori land was now not used for any effective functions – and modified into, therefore, being wasted.

The Europeans managed to acquire land and they right away located it to appropriate use. Because of such regulations and attitudes, by the point the twentieth century sprung a nook, the Maori had even much less than 15% of the lands that they used to have in 1840.

Other guidelines and laws to enhance the lives of people in New Zealand furthermore commenced out to be designed. These legal hints involved the vintage-age pension, the economic arbitration device, and the restrict in walking hours for more younger employees and women. These changes grew to become New Zealand right into a "operating man's paradise," further to a "social laboratory."

Chapter 15: Identity Emergence In New Zealand

Around 1886, the generations have modified over New Zealand. At this point, maximum of the non-Maori human beings that were residing in New Zealand had been already born and raised there. In the start, the term "New Zealander" modified into first associated with the Maori – however at this issue, all of it took a very new which means that that.

However, the identification of New Zealand have end up despite the fact that specially contained in the imperial identity. Since the economic ties were strong, the loyalty of the New Zealanders modified into strengthened – counting on an empire that allowed them to regular their place on this international.

Most of the Pakeha (non-Maori) still located themselves as British and could name Britain their "domestic." This loyalty modified into moreover obvious in 1899 of their enthusiasm to useful resource Britain in the Second Anglo Boer-War. This changed into truely the number one time that the troops from New Zeeland served distant places. Seddon furthermore proudly stated that the Empire's "pink tie" effective New Zealand to Britain, the "Mother Country."

In 1901, the Commonwealth of Australia were installation – however New Zealand refused to turn out to be a part of it and take the name of "6th usa of the usa." There were numerous reasons for rejecting the federation with Australia – and this turn out to be no longer only due to the fact they aspired for popularity, identity, and grand future. Many of the New Zealanders feared that their u . S . Can be positioned prone to social reforms that would disrupt the contemporary-day one, whereas different humans believed

New Zealand residents had been a "higher kind of British human beings."

Eventually, the federation in the long run strengthened the national identity and made the New Zealanders greater best of the truth that they need to not surrender their independence. Soon enough, symbols of their nationhood began to emerge – with a extremely-current flag in 1902 and the Coat of Arms in 1911.

In 1907, together with the British Empire, New Zealand have become a dominion. Many people stated that this can be a "skip up" as it joins the "faculty of British international places" – but real, exquisite little had changed. New Zealand have become no plenty much less or no extra impartial from Great Britain in comparison to even because it modified into fine a colony. It have become best the choice that had modified.

Chapter 16: The Era Of The Reform Party

No one changed into pretty able to wholesome the consecutive election victories that Richard Seddon, the exceptional great of New Zealand, managed to pull via. Indeed, on the identical time as he tipped over a hundred thirty kg (inflicting him to be known as "huge-than-existence"), his passing however got here as quite a surprise for the human beings of New Zealand.

The Falling of the Liberals

In many methods, Seddon changed into an act that changed into quite hard to comply with. His deputy, Joseph Ward, had come returned successful after important the Liberals via the 1908 elections – but he did not have the enchantment that Seddon had to the humans. Instead, he grow to be criticized for being "too verbose" and being "too preoccupied approximately his very very own profile and look."

In 1911, it have become quite clean that the citizens not had any interest inside the Liberals, and they had without a doubt grown bored with them. Without "King Dick" to assist enchantment to the hundreds, the undertaking become pretty hard – and it end up confirmed even as the Reform Party of William Massey had acquired four more seats.

Ward gave up his position due to the fact the leader of the Liberals and become changed by way of using Thomas Mackenzie – but even he turn out to be no longer capable of change the tides. By the center of July 1912, William Massey had grown effective sufficient to form his personal government.

"Farmer Bill" Massey

Massey's Reform Party had received some of help from farmers within the course of New Zealand. This became due to the truth those human beings desired to own the lands that they've been walking on – and that they have become irritated with the insurance of the Liberals to hire rather than to sell the land of the Crown. Plus, but the truth that Massey changed into furthermore nicknamed "Farmer Bill," he had acquired masses of assist from the -developing cities and cities within the North Island.

These people yearned for secondary/technical schooling, white-collar employment, and domestic possession. Plus, at the identical time as Massey himself end up certainly a farmer, loads of his Cabinet had been professionals or city businessmen.

The Liberal Party end up regularly criticized for manipulating the general public company through way of the usage of dishing out patronage. In an try to surrender this "political cronyism" and those "jobs for the men," the authorities of the Reform proceeded to installation the Public Service Commissioner. This unbiased service might be accountable for appointing, similarly to selling New Zealand's public servants.

The belief that the Reform Party modified into without a doubt a "Farmer's Party" end up likely a reaction to two vital sports in industrial enterprise New Zealand's history: The Waihi miner strike of 1912, and the general and waterfront moves of 1913. The u . S . Was break up into camps that had no way of reconciling with each extraordinary, and the authorities sided with the employers on the commercial militancy that adverse them. After an extended six-month strike from the miners' company, one of the putting miners, Fred Evans, come to be fatally injured in a conflict with the strike-breakers. Other violent clashes happened at the strike on the waterfront lines after severa business movements prevented the farmers from promoting their merchandise to the markets distant places.

The Massey Administration had Alexander Herdman and John Cullen to play a key role in this struggle. They enlisted masses of what they known as "special forces," lots of them being farmers on horseback, to defeat the militant labor and break the strike. This struggle that lasted for two months involved round sixteen,000 unionists recruited from all in the course of New Zealand — and determined a number of clashes maximum of the strikers and the ideal set up constables referred to as "Massey's Cossacks." The strike came to an cause December, with the United Federation of Labor being on the dropping crew.

Because of these moves, Massey acquired hundreds of hate from the city humans – hate that could be exceeded down through generations. On the other hand, the farmers saw him fame as "agency, and decisive," his intimidating and sturdy thoughts-set winning him loads of votes.

Chapter 17: New Zealand Goes Into War

Even as New Zealand have become enhancing from its very non-public wars, they still needed to play their element in the outer wars as well – especially if this benefitted them. In the 12 months 1909, Joseph Ward, the Prime Minister of New Zealand, announced that the country would fund the constructing of a battlecruiser. This choice modified into taken when Britain had perceived a chance from the Germans – and thinking about that a robust British Empire is vital for an extraordinary New Zealand safety.

Preparation for War

In order to make the HMS New Zealand, the New Zealand taxpayers needed to pay round £1.7 million (the equal of $270 million nowadays). When the supply come to be completed in 1913, it have become despatched to visit the whole dominion for 2 weeks – and about 500,000 New

Zealanders have come to investigate the present they made for Mother England.

In 1909, compulsory navy education was introduced in New Zealand. All boys which have been elderly among 12 and 14 needed to do fifty two hours of education each 12 months as a Junior Cadet. It have become essential for the empire that the citizens ought to grow healthy and healthful, within the occasion that they'll have to be known as out to struggle.

The kingdom moreover had the "Boy Scout Movement," delivered in 1908, which had quite masses the identical cause: growing patriots that have been capable of shielding the Empire. These boys might be educated about patriotism, values, region – but also can go through outside education via sports sports and video games.

Word of the First World War

On August 5, 1914, Wellington obtained phrase that Britain had long beyond into conflict. Just as they've got finished with the South African war, New Zealand have become feeling enthusiastic while Mother England known as New Zeeland to the hands. The fact that Germany attacked Belgium, a reasonably small u.S.A. Of america, struck every different nerve within the citizens of New Zealand.

Because of this, lots of human beings in New Zealand signed up to enter the provider, keen to be of use and decided no longer to miss out at the struggle that they anticipated to be over through Christmas with out many casualties. However, they have been pretty lengthy of their evaluation, because the warfare proved greater detrimental than they idea it might be.

In the give up, the First World War took the lives of approximately 18,500 New

Zealanders, and round 41,000 were critically injured. It sparked masses of debate whether or not this helped them forge their country wide identification or now not. What is high-quality, but, is that a few little-acknowledged places that have been hundreds of miles from their domestic (which includes Somme, Passchendaele, and Gallipoli) might probable all the time be etched into their memory.

Taking component in World War I had a first rate impact on New Zealand, no longer nice reshaping the perception that the us had of itself however moreover approximately the place that they occupy inside the international. Around one hundred,000 New Zealanders went remote places at warfare – and for most of them, this emerge as their first time. Many of these New Zealanders anticipated it like an journey – however in the long run, the fact grew to grow to be out to be pretty one-of-a-kind.

Now that they have been at this shape of great distance away, the New Zealanders were very privy to who they have been – and in which they've come from. They moreover had the capability to examine themselves with men from specific countries – whether it emerge as inside the lower back of the traces or in struggle. Because of those studies, they acquired their private enjoy of separate identification.

Going for World War II

As it become the case for maximum international places on the planet, World War II changed into additionally some detail that couldn't be prevented. The worldwide locations would nearly get roped in, siding on the frontline with the global locations they had been allied with.

New Zealand was, another time, no exception. The Dominion changed into called to war, in which they fought in assist for Britain. The mother u.S.A. Of the united states needed to be protected – particularly in the event that they preferred to grasp onto the safety of their very own u . S .. And judging from the beyond opinions, this need to now not had been a few problem hard to govern.

However, they'll soon see that the scenario seems as a substitute bleak. When Singapore fell, the self belief of the New Zealanders have emerge as shaken – and they no longer believed that Britain may additionally need to guarantee the security in their u . S . A ..

The bulk of the New Zealand forces had been efficiently stranded inside the Middle East and in Egypt – and it regarded like there has been no wish in sight for them at this issue. Still, ultimately, it became the united states that included New Zealand in opposition to the Japanese forces within the struggle on the Pacific.

The Second World War took away the lives of approximately eleven,625 from the complete of a hundred and forty,000 that served foreign places. This variety had made a large dent within the population of New Zealand – one that could take a reasonably long time to get over. In 1945, New Zealand again from the battle and started out to dress their (albeit high-quality) wounds.

Chapter 18: Expanding Cultural Diversity And Trade

New Zealand has commonly been a rustic full of cultural variety and shopping for and selling opportunities. Granted, this did not commonly occur while best the Maori inhabited the land – but in most instances, inside the destiny after the Europeans had arrived.

Trading Expansion

When Britain had turn out to be a part of the European Economic Community (an event which occurred in 1973), New Zealand had already began out to diversify its export exchange. Up until that point, New Zealand modified into most effective dealing with the markets of Britain – but that have become no longer some component possible to do, considering the occasions. If New Zealand wanted to acquire fulfillment in the long run, they had to change their taxes and diversify their markets.

The Vogel plan helped in those events. Granted, a number of the buying and promoting grow to be finished via deliver – however way to the apparition of the modern day railways, shopping for and selling may be executed via land as nicely. Whether it became on the short or the lengthy distance, New Zealand now had opened the gates to a in particular immoderate type of countries.

By the time the 20th century came to an give up, New Zealand had widened its outlook. Exports had been performed to a much broader sort of international places, and the monetary system started out out to decorate. Farmed items had been notwithstanding the reality that the precept trading options, however there has been a number of artisanal items that made New Zealand an appealing choice for consumers.

Expanding Cultural Diversity

In the start, there were organizations: the Maori and the British. However, with time, the life-style had moreover come to be greater numerous. In the Nineteen Eighties, a immoderate kind of ethnic agencies came to New Zealand, looking for settlement – and were encouraged by the use of the paintings possibilities that saved arising.

Now, New Zealand is a as an opportunity multicultural u . S .. According to the data taken from the national Census of 2013, 25% of the humans that have settled in New Zealand had been born in one-of-a-kind global locations, 7% have been from the islands within the Pacific, 12% of them had been Asian, and 15% were the Maori. The relaxation were part of the European settlers that at the start got here to the land – born and raised right here, as a legacy from the number one colonies.

English, Maori, and Samoan stay the maximum not unusual languages to be spoken in New Zealand – however Hindu is likewise pretty not unusual. Given how matters are going now, it is predicted that New Zealand can also further boom its cultural range.

Historical Places to See in New Zealand

New Zealand within reason lots even though known as a "younger" u . S . – however in reality, there's masses of records backing this u.S. Up. Its records spreads over complete centuries, from the immediately the Maori first came to the land, observed via the British who colonized the location. If you need to get a firsthand experience of the statistics of

New Zealand, here are a few net web sites that you may need to go to.

The Stone Store and the Mission House, Kerikeri

The Mission House – occasionally known as the Kemp House – is one among New Zealand's oldest surviving homes. Built in 1821-1822 in Kerikeri, this form end up initially a venture house, after which it have emerge as the house of the Kemp family. Nearby, you can find the Stone Store, this is (manifestly) the oldest stone constructing that has survived through records. It is an appropriate region to visit in case you are inquisitive about the proper shape.

The Treaty House, Waitangi

The Treaty of Waitangi is the file on which New Zealand modified into almost based totally – in particular, on February sixth, 1840. So, truely, considering the importance of this file, you may want to visit the actual area wherein each model of it became signed.

The Treaty of Waitangi has brought on loads of dialogue, by using way of and large due to the fact no longer each signer understood the first-rate clauses of what they had been signing for. Even so, considering the significance of the report, a go to to the Treaty House is probably a few detail you need to don't forget which includes in your itinerary.

The "Queen Victoria" Statue, Auckland

New Zealand became a colony with quite an lousy lot its private identification and assets – however we can't forget about about the truth that it grow to be but in near relation with Great Britain. They have been loyal to the Queen, and the Crown have to notwithstanding the truth that ship beneficial aid at the same time as the colony asked it. This is why the revealing of Queen Victoria's statue held this form of exquisite which means to their history.

On the overdue Queen's birthday, humans could acquire and have an fantastic time within the the front of the statue and will have a laugh what emerge as called "Empire Day" – a holiday that could finally emerge as "Commonwealth Day." The holiday changed into as quickly as held on May twenty fourth, however it is not honestly practiced – and has almost disappeared from the calendar. Still, paying a go to to the statue of Queen Victoria is a few issue that is nicely well worth doing.

Pencarrow Lighthouse, Wellington

Being the primary everlasting lighthouse in New Zealand, the Pencarrow lighthouse is all once more a form this is actually in reality worth seeing. Plus, it turned into the awesome lighthouse that had a girl as its eternal keeper – a woman named Mary Bennett.

Mary first operated the lighthouse on January 1st, 1859. Bennett once more to England in 1865, the lighthouse being decommissioned – with the Baring Head lighthouse task its characteristic. Still, the lighthouse remains status, and vacationers are welcome to go to this piece of information if they'll be ever near Wellington Harbor.

Basin Reserve, Wellington

At some issue in 1855, there was a shallow swamp in Wellington that have come to be intended for use as a dock. However, an earthquake tired this swamp – so, in preference to turning it proper right into a dock like it have become planned, they made it proper into a undertaking reserve. In 1863, community prisoners have been used for filling that internet net page – erecting a grandstand some years later.

The citizen committee decreed that this place may be a cricket ground – and that has actually become its fundamental use. However, this region is likewise on occasion used for severa events, sports sports sports activities – even royal and political visits. Considering that that is moreover the location in which the primary royal show of power befell, it's far nicely honestly worth seeing in case you are seeking out historical internet websites.

www.ingramcontent.com/pod-product-compliance
Lightning Source LLC
Chambersburg PA
CBHW071442080526
44587CB00014B/1955